NINA MAE McKINNEY

THE BLACK GARBO

STEPHEN BOURNE

Published in the USA by:
BearManor Media
PO Box 1129
Duncan, Oklahoma 73534-1129
www.bearmanormedia.com

ISBN 978-1-59393-658-7

Printed in the United States of America.
Book design by Brian Pearce | Red Jacket Press.

TABLE OF CONTENTS

ACKNOWLEDGEMENTS

Thanks go to Donald Bogle and Charlene Regester for their work on Nina Mae McKinney and acknowledgement of her pioneering contribution to popular cinema (see Bibliography).

Thanks to Ron Geesin, Phyllis C. Benton (Midnight Ramble Video) and to the jazz historian Howard Rye for sharing his detailed work on Nina Mae McKinney and Garland Wilson's European appearances in the 1930s. Rye's published work includes "Visiting Fireman: 11: Garland Wilson" in *Storyville* (119), June-July 1985, pp 176-193.

Thanks to the genealogist Debbie Montgomerie who has uncovered some important and interesting facts about Nina Mae McKinney's genealogy, early years and travels to Europe.

All photographs are from the author's private collection unless otherwise noted.

Though every care has been taken, if, through inadvertence or failure to trace the present owners, we have included any copyright material without acknowledgement or permission, we offer our apologies to all concerned.

INTRODUCTION

IN 1929, WHEN NINA MAE MCKINNEY MADE HER SCREEN debut in *Hallelujah*, Richard Watts, Jr., the film critic for the *New York Herald Tribune*, described her as "assuredly one of the most beautiful women of our time." Five years later, Richard Watts, Jr. rediscovered Nina Mae singing in a "swanky nightclub" in Athens, Greece. She was billed as "The Black Greta Garbo." Consequently he wrote a glowing appraisal of her in the *New York Herald Tribune* (see Appendix for a transcript of the complete article). He also criticized Hollywood for not making use of her. Nina Mae was beautiful, talented and, after her screen debut in 1929, a promising career in the movies was in the cards. However, it didn't happen. Nina Mae discovered that Hollywood — and America — was not ready for a black leading lady. The only roles she could expect to play were scatterbrained maids to white stars, but that didn't happen either. So Nina Mae travelled to Europe and enjoyed a few triumphs as a singer and star of vaudeville theatres, mostly in Britain, where she based herself in the mid-1930s. However, this dynamic and gorgeous star was quickly forgotten, forced into the shadows of Hollywood history. She was pushed aside when younger black actresses sought fame and fortune in the movie capital. In the 1940s it was Lena Horne. In the 1950s it was Dorothy Dandridge. In the 1940s, when Lena signed the first long-term (seven-year) film contract with a major studio (M-G-M), Nina Mae was reduced to playing the maid stereotype she had successfully avoided. In the 1950s, when Dorothy became the first African American star to be nominated for a Best Actress Oscar (for *Carmen Jones*), Nina Mae hardly worked at all, and became a tragic figure.

In his *Encyclopedia of African American Actresses in Film and Television* (2010), Bob McCann described Nina Mae as a "seminal black actress" who "deserves rediscovery in the way that icons such as Anna May Wong and Josephine Baker have been reassessed and rediscovered. Although Nina Mae McKinney didn't have the opportunity to develop a formidable filmography, her role in King Vidor's *Hallelujah* and surviving footage of her song and dance routines shows that she was a major talent."

So Lena Horne and Dorothy Dandridge, not Nina Mae, are acknowledged as the first black women to be given star status in American cinema but, in spite of their beauty and talent, they discovered the same situation that Nina Mae found in the early 1930s. Opportunities to play starring roles in Hollywood movies were few and far between. Nevertheless they did make an impact in films. Lena was memorable as the beautiful seductress Georgia Brown in M-G-M's *Cabin in the Sky* (1943) and, as *Carmen Jones* (1954), Dorothy gave a magnificent performance as a tempestuous, flamboyant hell raiser. In addition to their own autobiographies, Lena and Dorothy's lives and careers have been documented in several biographies including James Gavin's *Stormy Weather–The Life of Lena Horne* (2009) and Donald Bogle's *Dorothy Dandridge — A Biography* (1997). With such attention, it would be easy to assume that they were the first African American women to achieve stardom in Hollywood but, before Lena and Dorothy, there was Nina Mae.

Nina Mae found fame in Hollywood (and America) right at the beginning of the sound era, and then made a brief impact in British films, including a co-starring role opposite Paul Robeson in *Sanders of the River* (1935). However, in spite of her success, she is often overlooked in histories of cinema. She is conspicuous by her absence in the several editions of Ephraim Katz's *The Macmillan International Film Encyclopedia* (first published in 1994), advertised on its front cover as *"The most comprehensive one volume encyclopedia of world cinema."* However, Nina Mae's brief career (three feature films) in British cinema of the 1930s is acknowledged with an entry for the actress in Brian McFarlane's *The Encyclopedia of British Film* (2003). In spite of a cult following, which is growing all the time, and demonstrated by fans who post enthusiastic comments about Nina Mae on the internet, including IMDB (The Internet Movie Database) and YouTube, it is only on rare occasions that she is given formal recognition as the screen's first black movie star. Her contribution to cinema, both in America and Britain, should be better known, and acknowledged. So far, African American writers like Donald Bogle in his many books, including *Bright Boulevards, Bold Dreams — The Story of Black Hollywood* (2005), and Charlene Regester in a chapter dedicated to Nina Mae in *African American Actresses — The Struggle for Visibility, 1900-1960* (2010), have helped enormously to give Nina Mae her rightful place in cinema history. It is hoped that this modest tribute will also make an important contribution.

I first came across the name Nina Mae McKinney in Peter Noble's *The Negro in Films* (1948) — a British publication, and one of the earliest studies of black cinema. I discovered a second-hand copy of this book as a teenager in London in the early 1970s. Noble doesn't say much about her except that she was an "extremely lovely" dancer who found that Hollywood had no real place for her. Soon afterwards I broadened my knowledge and appreciation of black movie actors when I purchased Donald Bogle's pioneer study, *Toms, Coons, Mulattoes, Mammies & Bucks — An Interpretive History of Blacks in American Films* (1973). Bogle's groundbreaking book updated and extended Noble's pioneering work, and taught me everything I needed to know at that time about the black stars of Hollywood. Bogle acknowledged that Nina Mae was the first black movie star. However, Nina Mae spent the rest of her life hoping for another big movie success. It did not happen. Although she couldn't have known it in 1929, Nina Mae became the first black star to learn a hard lesson: after one successful film appearance, there were no follow-up roles. In 1929 Hollywood was not ready to promote a black leading lady in films. It could be argued this is a situation that still exists today.

I also heard about Nina Mae from an aunt and uncle who went to see her at the London Palladium in September 1933. She had obviously made an impression, because in the 1970s they were still enthusing about her, and what a great performance she had given. I can recall when I first saw Nina Mae on screen. As a teenager in the early 1970s I saw her on television in the 1949 film *Pinky*. A few years later, in 1977, I glimpsed her briefly in archive footage in a BBC television documentary called *The Birth of Television*. In the early 1980s, after I had become a member of the National Film Theatre in London, I made sure I attended screenings of her first film, *Hallelujah, Safe in Hell* (in a retrospective of the Hollywood director William A. Wellman) and, in 1982, *Sanders of the River* (in a season of films based on the novels of Edgar Wallace). In 1988 Donald Bogle's excellent television series *Brown Sugar* was shown in Britain, and he included a memorable tribute to Nina Mae at the end of programme one. This featured some rare and captivating archive film of Nina Mae at the height of her fame in the 1930s. It left the viewer wondering why she didn't do more film work. Meanwhile, I found out as much as I could about Nina Mae from the files of the British Film Institute's library, the BBC Written Archives, and my growing collection of books about African American cinema. I also searched for–and found — some rare photos of Nina Mae at various movie memorabilia fairs, and the sorely missed Cinema Bookshop in London's West End.

I soon felt confident to write my own appraisal of Nina Mae's film career, but an early attempt was rejected. In 1984 I proposed a tribute to Nina Mae to the popular monthly British film magazine *Photoplay*, but the editor turned me down. I still have the rejection letter from the magazine's deputy editor (dated April 17, 1984). She said: "Many thanks for your letter and article "Black Garbo" which I read with interest, as did my editor. Unfortunately we feel that it is slightly too "heavy" for *Photoplay*, and even with editing down, somewhat obscure for our mainly youthful readership. I'm afraid that on this particular magazine we have to stick to more well known names like Eddie Murphy and Richard Pryor." Five years later the opportunity to write an article about Nina Mae came with a commission to write about her film career in the American journal *Films in Review* (January/February 1991). Twenty years later, after several publishers rejected the proposal, BearManor Media agreed to publish this book to commemorate Nina Mae's centenary in June 2012, but it will not be as comprehensive as I would like. Information about Nina Mae has been hard to find. Most of what is available is contradictory, sketchy and unsubstantiated, but it has been a labour of love worth labouring over. Nina Mae is a star who should not have been forgotten.

AUTHOR'S NOTE ABOUT "THE BLACK GARBO"

IN THE 1920S AND 1930S IT WAS COMMON PRACTICE FOR most African American stars of "race movies" (see Chapter 6) to be named after a famous white Hollywood movie star. So Lorenzo Tucker was known as "The Black Valentino", Ethel Moses as the 'Negro [Jean] Harlow' and Bee Freeman was "The Sepia Mae West". When Nina Mae McKinney's film career was launched in 1929, she was likened to the "It" girl, Clara Bow and even named the 'dusky Clara Bow' by some but, in 1934, when she visited Europe for cabaret engagements, she was billed as "The Black Garbo". The title stuck, but in reality Nina Mae had little in common with Greta Garbo, the intense, melancholy Swedish star of M-G-M melodramas such as *Anna Christie* and *Queen Christina*. Garbo and McKinney were breathtakingly beautiful, but their screen personas couldn't have been more different. Beauty and talent were the only things they had in common.

In today's more enlightened times, some may feel uncomfortable with the naming of black movie stars after white stars because no one would have called Jean Harlow the "white Nina Mae McKinney". However, this was the way some black stars were identified and promoted for the general public in the 1930s, especially those who starred in 'race movies'. So the title "The Black Garbo" has remained with Nina since those appearances in Europe in 1934.

CHAPTER 1

NINA MAE'S EARLY LIFE

1912-1932

NINA MAE MCKINNEY WAS BORN NANNIE MAYME MCKINNEY on June 16, 1912 in Lancaster, South Carolina. The actual date of her birth has not been confirmed. A copy of her birth certificate has not been located and put into the public domain, but the date given here is likely to be the most accurate (see Author's note at the end of this chapter). One of the earliest surviving known records is the March 1931 passenger list from Le Havre, France to New York in which eighteen-year-old "Nina McKinney" entered June 16, 1912 as her date of birth, and Lancaster, South Carolina as her place of birth.

Nina Mae was the daughter of Hal and Georgia McKinney. She was just a child when her parents left Lancaster for New York City. The McKinneys left their daughter in the care of her great-aunt, Carrie Sanders, until she was a teenager. In Lancaster, Nina Mae's "Aunt Carrie" lived in a small apartment on the large South Carolina estate of Colonel Leroy Springs, a successful white businessman who owned Springs Industries. Carrie worked as a cook and housekeeper for the Springs family. As a child, Nina Mae ran errands for Lena Jones Springs who presented her with a bicycle to ride to the local post office to collect mail for the family. Legend has it that Nina Mae impressed the locals with her riding stunts. She attended the all-black Lancaster Industrial School (founded by Colonel Springs), where she took part in school plays. She was about twelve or thirteen-years-old when she left Lancaster to join her parents in New York City. Her father worked for the U. S. Postal Service. In New York City Nina Mae attended Public School 126 in Lower Manhattan and, unlike the rural South where she had been growing up, discovered more opportunities to see stage productions and films. In fact, Nina Mae had been stage struck from an early age, and the young girl taught herself to dance by imitating dancers she saw on the stage and in silent films. After she left school, Nina Mae joined the chorus line of Lew Leslie's hit Broadway show *Blackbirds of 1928*.

No documentation exists to confirm when Nina Mae joined the chorus of *Blackbirds of 1928*. Her name does not appear amongst the chorines in the original cast that was published in the programme for the first performance at the Liberty Theatre on May 9, 1928. Perhaps she joined later, as a chorus line replacement. The show's white producer, Lew Leslie, had been planning to star Florence Mills in this new edition of *Blackbirds*. Mills had been the star of Leslie's famous London edition of 1926. However, Mills's sudden death on November 1, 1927 meant that Leslie had to reorganise the show, with singers Adelaide Hall and Aida Ward taking the leads. The tap dancer Bill 'Bojangles' Robinson was hired during the out-of-town tryout. A knockout score by Jimmy McHugh (music) and Dorothy Fields (lyrics) included "I Can't Give You Anything But Love." With such talent involved, *Blackbirds of 1928* became the most successful *Blackbirds* production and the longest-running all-black cast revue in Broadway theatre history. Bill Robinson was a great success with his appearance in the second act, performing "Doin' the New Low-Down". Audiences loved him, and he went on to Hollywood stardom in the 1930s in four Shirley Temple films. "Diga Diga Doo" was introduced by Adelaide Hall and a chorus of beautiful chorines in red sequins in a pseudo-African jungle setting. Hall later recalled: "I hardly wore anything at all, just beads and feathers. It upset my family very much. Especially my mother! I didn't see anything wrong with it. I was young and enjoying myself." After a record-breaking 518 performances on Broadway, in 1929 Adelaide — without Bill — travelled with the show for a triumphant run at the Moulin Rouge in Paris. Nina Mae was not in the cast, either, for she had received an offer she couldn't refuse.

Legend has it that Nina Mae was just sixteen when she was plucked from the *Blackbirds* chorus by King Vidor, one of Hollywood's top directors, and offered the lead in his film *Hallelujah* (1929) (see Chapter 2). It sounds like a story straight from a Hollywood movie, and nothing has come to light about the production number in which Vidor noticed Nina Mae. Vidor later recalled in his autobiography *A Tree is a Tree* (1953): "She was third from the right in the chorus. She was beautiful and talented and glowing with personality."

After starring in *Hallelujah* Nina Mae discovered there was no place in Hollywood at that time for a black leading lady. So she followed in the footsteps of the African American singer and dancer Josephine Baker and left the United States for Europe. In 1925 Baker became the toast of Paris with her appearance in the stage production *La Revue Negre* and thereafter based herself in France. Throughout the 1920s and 1930s Paris — and other European cities — became a haven for African American entertainers and musicians. They experienced less racism, and more opportunities for work, and black women like Baker, Adelaide Hall, Valaida Snow, Elisabeth Welch and Mabel Mercer (from England) captured the continent with their songs, beauty, elegance and style. The blues singer Alberta Hunter later recalled: "The Negro artists went to Europe because we were given a chance. In Europe they had your name up in lights. People in the United States would not give us that chance."

Eighteen-year-old Nina Mae sailed for Europe on the S.S. *Bremen* on December 5, 1930 for a three-month tour of personal appearances with

Hallelujah. In America the press covered her departure, noting that she wore a black satin and black velvet coat trimmed with fox, and carrying a huge bouquet of chrysanthemums. In Europe she also sang and danced in cafes and nightclubs, including a three week engagement at L'il Trianon in Paris, four weeks in Berlin, one week in Cannes, and additional appearances in Belgrade, Monte Carlo, Serbia and London. Nina Mae reportedly earned $1,000 a week. In January 1931 she was featured in Berlin's 'Kabarett der Komiker'. She departed for the United States at Le Havre on the French Line's M.S. *Lafayette* and arrived in New York City on March 20, 1931. On the U. S. Passenger List, Nina Mae entered her address as 365 Lenox Avenue, Apartment 5, New York City.

When Nina Mae returned to Paris in December 1932, she was accompanied by the jazz pianist Garland Wilson, but he later claimed that their cabaret appearance at the famous Chez Florence nightclub was a "flop" and increased his dislike of France (he spoke no French). Nina Mae and Wilson stayed together for several years (see Chapter 3). They recorded two songs in Paris in December: Harold Arlen and Ted Koehler's "Minnie the Moocher's Wedding Day" and Clarence Williams's "Rhapsody in Love". The 1932 recordings reveal Nina Mae's early promise as a singer in the jazz idiom and in 1985, when Laurie Wright reviewed a Garland Wilson compilation for the jazz journal *Storyville*, his appraisal of their two recordings from 1932 acknowledges her jazz style: "He had a long-time professional association with Nina Mae McKinney and no doubt the coupling here gives a fair idea of the type of thing they did together. He is indeed a superb accompanist, sensitive to both the lyrics and the singer's needs and Nina Mae is an above-average vocalist with a pleasantly husky delivery, dropping into a growl for effect, but who makes use of some odd pronunciations; more often than not, the word 'rhapsody' comes out sounding like 'rhapsoday' on their second title ["Rhapsody in Love"]."

Although she continued to sing jazz numbers throughout the 1930s and 1940s in her cabaret and vaudeville acts, Nina Mae has never been properly acknowledged in the jazz world. John Chilton included an entry for her in his *Who's Who of Jazz* (1970), but she is not mentioned in two comprehensive studies of women in jazz: Linda Dahl's *Stormy Weather — The Music and Lives of a Century of Jazz Women* (1984) and Sally Placksin's *Jazzwomen 1900 to the Present — Their Words, Lives and Music* (1985). However, the reason for this could be Nina Mae's lack of recording output. Her 1932 Paris recordings with Garland Wilson are the only ones to be verified. In spite of her popularity in Britain in the 1930s, she did not make any recordings in that country. In America in the 1930s and 1940s she did not enjoy the recording output of her African American contemporaries, namely Ethel Waters, Billie Holiday, and Ella Fitzgerald, in spite of sharing their popularity, especially in the African American community. All that survives of Nina Mae's singing are her two recordings and the songs she performed in her American and British films (1929 to 1939).

The 1932 Paris recordings may not have been Nina Mae's first. In 1928 Alice Clinton, who is probably Nina Mae using a pseudonym, recorded two vaudeville blues numbers: "Do What You Did Last Night" by Andy Razaf and J. C. Johnson and "(Since You've Been Gone) There's Been Some Changes Made". In an email to the author dated February 27, 2011, the jazz historian Howard Rye explains: "The recordings were made around April 20, 1928. For Gennett recordings made in New York City we only have the date on which the masters were received at headquarters in Richmond, IN. It's unlikely there is a constant relationship between the recording session, the date the masters were packed up, and the transit time, so we can only guess how many days earlier they were made. J.C. Johnson, who is the pianist, said it was Nina Mae. In the nature of the case it is impossible to verify this. She is Alice Clinton in the Gennett filing so Johnson brought her in under the pseudonym; if that is what it is. The recordings are available on the Compact Disc *Female Blues Singers Volume 4 1921-1930* (Document DOCD5508). I just played them again and I feel what I felt last time I did it. It could be, but it doesn't leap out at you. The recording is fairly bawdy which may provide a motive for the pseudonym on the part of a singer who was trying break through to white time. 'Changes Made' is not the well-known 'There'll Be Some Changes Made.'"

AUTHOR'S NOTE

Nina's year of birth has sometimes been given as 1913, but it is more than likely to be 1912. When she travelled from Plymouth to New York in December 1934, Nina Mae entered her name as "Nina Monroe." She claimed to be married to Jimmy Monroe at the time (for more information on Monroe see Chapter 6). She entered Lancaster, South Carolina as her place of birth, and 1912 as the year in which she was born. When she arrived in Glasgow, Scotland from New York on March 30, 1936, "Nina Mae McKinney" gave her age as twenty-three. In the 1920 United States census her name is entered as Nannie M. McKenna, age eight, which also suggests a 1912 year of birth.

CHAPTER 2

HALLELUJAH
AND
HOLLYWOOD

1929-1932

IN HOLLYWOOD KING VIDOR WAS ONE OF M-G-M'S TOP directors, with a list of impressive movie classics to his name. These included the silents *The Big Parade* (1925), *The Crowd* (1928) and *Show People* (1928). He had directed some of the silent era's greatest female stars, including Lillian Gish and Marion Davies and, by the end of the 1920s, Vidor could write his own ticket. M-G-M would support any film project he wanted to develop and he chose a subject that hadn't been attempted before: a serious feature film about the lives of African Americans. *Hallelujah* would also be his first sound film. M-G-M executives were reluctant to commit to this idea. They were convinced that a film with an African American cast would be barred from the all-white cinemas of the southern states. Determined to make the film, Vidor offered to part-finance *Hallelujah* with his fee, as long as M-G-M matched his contribution. The reply came back from M-G-M mogul Nicholas Schenck: "If that's the way you feel about it, I'll let you make a picture about whores."

Vidor planned *Hallelujah* as a semi-musical that he hoped would avoid racial stereotyping. The story, though melodramatic, was kept simple: Zeke, a black Southern cotton farm worker, goes to town to sell his family's cotton crop, but he is seduced by the beautiful temptress Chick, a dancer and streetwise hussy of ill-repute. She convinces him to gamble his money, but the crap game is crooked and he is cheated out of $100, all the money he received for the crop. In his anger, Zeke accidently shoots and kills his younger brother. When he returns to his family, Zeke has found God and become a preacher, but when Chick comes to him to be "saved", he is again seduced by the immoral young woman.

Originally Vidor wanted Paul Robeson to play the leading role of Zeke. However, Robeson had settled in Britain and was enjoying success on the London stage in the musical *Show Boat*. Instead he cast Daniel L. Haynes, who had been an understudy for Jules Bledsoe in the original 1927 New York production of *Show Boat*. Vidor wanted the great jazz singer Ethel Waters for the role of Chick, but he didn't get her, either. She later complained in her autobiography *His Eye is on the Sparrow* (1951) that she lost the opportunity to star in *Hallelujah* because "the talent man King Vidor sent East to wave gold bags at me was stalled on the job by coloured theatrical people unfriendly to me." With Waters out of the frame, Vidor cast Honey Brown, who was described in early press releases as a "Harlem cabaret singer". Honey's chance for movie fame ended when she had to leave the cast because of illness. Nina Mae McKinney was a last-minute replacement.

In an interview with Nancy Dowd in *King Vidor* (1988), the director explained that most of the supporting cast were found in the "Negro" districts of Chicago and New York: "In Chicago we went to Negro Baptist churches, listening to choirs and talking to the people. They had to be able to sing well because we intended to use their actual voices. We also went to Negro nightclubs, always looking for people to cast. I saw a man standing on a street corner in Chicago and thought he was a fine type for the minister father." The man "standing on a street corner" was Harry Gray, an eighty-six year old ex-slave who was working as a porter. Vidor added: "Then we moved on to New York, rented a hall, and sent out word that we were looking for Negro people from the stage and choruses."

According to Frances E. Williams, in her tribute to Nina Mae in *Cinema — Women and Film* (1976), on her arrival at the M-G-M studio in Hollywood, the young woman was given the red carpet treatment: "limousine, studio suite, decorated dressing room, hairdresser, and wardrobe person." However, there was nothing to protect her from racist abuse. During the filming of *Hallelujah* it was rumoured that Nina Mae almost quit the production after a "grip" (a lighting and rigging technician) called her "nigger."

When the African American columnist Ruby Goodwin wrote a feature about Nina Mae in the *Pittsburgh Courier* (June 8, 1929), she said: "Miss McKinney's success came at an age when most girls are dreaming. She is only 16 years of age and for all her sophistication, is still a child who wants the admiration of the world. She is not haughty. She is modest and despite her phenomenal success carries no air of affectation."

In the film, Nina Mae is a revelation as the child-like but reckless Chick. Her natural, untrained acting, combined with her raw, unsophisticated but captivating singing and dancing, as well as her charisma, resulted in a fresh and exuberant performance. In his autobiography, *A Tree is a Tree* (1953), Vidor praised Nina Mae, and described his association with her: "It took no great effort to bring it out. She just had it, whatever you wanted, whatever you visualized, she could do it. Nina was full of life, full of expression, and just a joy to work with. Someone like her inspires a director."

In addition to the many spirituals used throughout the film, two new songs were composed for the stars of *Hallelujah* by one of America's greatest songwriters: Irving Berlin. The folk like "Waitin' at the End of the Road" was performed by Daniel L. Haynes and other plantation workers who were "ghosted" off-camera by the Dixie Jubilee Singers). Nina Mae sang Berlin's lively and under-rated (because it isn't mentioned in any of his biographies) "Swanee Shuffle" in the dive, backed by Curtis Mosby and his jazz band. The latter has stood the test of time, and Nina Mae's delivery of the song (and dance) is wonderful.

In fact, throughout *Hallelujah*, Nina Mae's performance is a captivating star turn. In 1988 Donald Bogle described her in *Blacks in American Films and Television — An Illustrated Encyclopedia*: "McKinney, the actress, is energy incarnate and delirious fun to watch...whose fearlessly kinetic Swanee Shuffle is a predecessor to the break dance maneuvers of the 1980s. Her sexiness is always endearingly girlish and innocent. When Vidor becomes too high-falutingly moody and serious, McKinney shows up and lets us see how black energy can send a picture into a heady tailspin."

Most contemporary critics praised the film, but there were some who hated it. In *The First Hollywood Musicals* (1996), Edwin M. Bradley compares two distinctly contrasting reviews. Richard Watts, Jr., described it as "one of the great motion pictures, a work to be compared, with unabashed enthusiasm, to such a foreign classic as the mighty *Potemkin*. It is poetry, drama and pictorial magnificence, combined in one stalwart whole...It is the talking picture made into a distinctive American dramatic form." However, the English critic James Agate disagreed and complained "Personally I don't care if it took Mr. Vidor 10 years to train these niggers. All I know is that 10 minutes is all I can stand of nigger ecstasy."

In *From Sambo to Superspade — The Black Experience in Motion Pictures* (1975), Daniel J. Leab commented: "There can be no doubt that Vidor's intentions were high-minded, and that he sincerely wanted to make a movie that would treat the black seriously. Vidor, however, proved unable to escape his Texas upbringing or then-common beliefs about blacks. As he said it was the 'sincerity and fervour of their religious expression' that had attracted him, as had 'the honest simplicity of their sexual drives'; he had concluded that 'the intermingling of these two activities seemed to offer strikingly dramatic content'...Vidor's film was actually a lumpy mixture of naive sentimentality and hackneyed melodrama." Leab adds that this misrepresentation aroused hostility amongst some African Americans and he quotes Paul Robeson who claimed the film was spoiled for him because "they took the Negro and his church services and made them funny."

In 1977 Thomas Cripps summarised *Hallelujah* in *Slow Fade to Black — The Negro in American Film, 1900-1942*. He said the film "neatly caught the piety and enthusiasm of rural religion, while only occasionally lapsing into stereotyped gamblers and mammies." A few years later Ethan Mordden enthused in *The Hollywood Musical* (1981): "Vidor's uncanny ability to duplicate existence instead of stylizing it makes *Hallelujah* the forerunner of the Italian neo-realist cinema of the 1940s and 1950s. And he has a better sense of tempo than Visconti and better actors than Rossellini." However, the African American viewpoint was best summarized by Donald Bogle who, in his pioneering study of black Hollywood, *Toms, Coons, Mulattoes, Mammies & Bucks* (1973), said Vidor used the black actors as "pawns": "used for an expression of his own feeling for mood and atmosphere rather than for any comment of their own." Bogle added that *Hallelujah* was the first and, for decades, the last Hollywood film to depict black family life in America's rural south. Bogle said it is "directly related to subsequent black family dramas such as *The Learning Tree* (1969) and *Sounder* (1972)." Forty years after *Hallelujah*, Gordon Parks's *The Learning Tree* was acknowledged as the first Hollywood film to be directed by a black director.

Nina Mae's character has been held up as an example of Hollywood stereotyping. In *Hallelujah* the dark-skinned Missy Rose, played by the blue singer Victoria Spivey, is the faithful fiancée from back home. She is dumped by Zeke after he is seduced by the amoral hussy Chick. The two women are contrasted by the clothes they wear: Missy Rose is a sexless frump, while Chick's attire — her slinky, tight-fitting dress, jewellery — enhances her attractiveness and vibrant sexuality. In 1973 Donald Bogle commented: "Chick represented the black woman as an exotic sex object, half woman, half child. She was the black woman out of control of her emotions, split in two by her loyalties and her own vulnerabilities."

Nina Mae's appearance in this film, and its importance to the African American community, was later immortalized in a short story by Langston Hughes, the African American literary giant of the Harlem Renaissance. In one of the stories in his "Simple" series, entitled *The Moon*, Simple recalls how he used to fall in love with movie stars when he was a young boy, "and you know I could not get near no movie star, they being white and way up yonder on the screen and me in a Jim Crow balcony down in Virginia. When I come to Baltimore as a young man, setting in a Jim Crow theatre on Pennsylvania Avenue, the first coloured movie star I fell in love with was Nina Mae McKinney, who was showing herself off in a picture called *Hallelujah*, which were fine. Nina Mae was so beautiful she made my heart ache." *The Moon* can be found in *The Collected Works of Langston Hughes Volume 8 — The Later Simple Stories* (2001).

After completing *Hallelujah*, M-G-M allegedly signed Nina Mae to a five-year contract, but they gave her only one assignment: *They Learned About Women* (1930). She made a brief and uncredited appearance in the "Harlem Madness" production number. Nina Mae then found herself in a Hollywood that had no place for her. In the early 1930s only a handful of African American actresses could find work in the movies, and these were mostly in stereotypical roles. Apart from Nina Mae, the most prominent at this time was Gertrude Howard who played the faithful mammy, Aunt Chloe, in the 1927 screen version of Harriet Beecher Stowe's *Uncle Tom's Cabin*. Howard subsequently found herself typecast as a mammy in a succession of films, including the first film version of *Show Boat* (1929) and *Hearts in Dixie* (1929). In her most famous role, as Mae West's scatterbrained maid and confidante Beulah Thorndike in *I'm No Angel* (1933), she is tossed one of the most infamous racist remarks ever made to a black woman in the movies: "Beulah, peel me a grape." Following Howard's unexpected death in 1934, Louise Beavers and Hattie McDaniel inherited — and shared — Howard's crown as Hollywood's favourite mammy but, unlike Howard, these gifted actresses defied convention and resisted the stereotype, but it was tough going. Describing Hollywood in the 1930s, Gary Null in *Black Hollywood* (1975) commented: "The black actors who became popular movie stars were still relegated to demeaning roles. Hollywood may have been aware of the new black middle class, but the stock black characters were poor shanty dwellers or comic servants."

However, there was a breakthrough in 1931 when the director William A. Wellman cast Nina Mae as the hotel waitress on a Caribbean island who befriends a runaway prostitute from New Orleans (Dorothy Mackaill) in his melodrama *Safe in Hell* (released as *The Lost Lady* in Britain). Frank T. Thompson in *William A. Wellman* (1983) explained that "One notable item about the film is the presence of two popular black actors, Nina Mae McKinney and Clarence Muse. In a period when blacks were so often exploited and stereotyped, these two characters are refreshingly positive; they may, in fact, be the only two reputable people in the film." The script is a white writer's idea of how African Americans spoke. On screen, however, this does not happen. In an extremely rare occasion in 1930s Hollywood, black characters were not forced to speak Hollywood's stereotypical version of African American dialect. One example of this alteration is given by Thomas Cripps in *Slow Fade to Black*. One of Nina Mae's lines was written in the script as "I'se a N'Orleans lady mahself" but on screen she says "I'm a New Orleans lady too." Says Frank T. Thompson:

"Either McKinney and Muse had enough clout to demand that they speak in normal language or Wellman just wanted to avoid a convenient cliché." Clarence Muse had a long career in Hollywood, starting in the 1920s and lasting until the 1970s. In an interview towards the end of his life, dated January 6, 1972, and published in *Every Step a Struggle — Interviews with Seven who Shaped the African-American Image in Movies* by Frank Manchel (2007), Muse told interviews Bob Sye and Ena Muse: "I did *Safe in Hell* with her. I did a West Indian running a hotel thing. Terrific picture. She's a terrific artist. More ought to be done about Nina Mae McKinney, because she did a magnificent job in that first picture [*Hallelujah*]."

When no further opportunities to work in Hollywood were forthcoming, Nina Mae prolonged her American movie career by appearing in a musical short, directed by Roy Mack, called *Pie Pie Blackbird* (1932). Her co-stars were Eubie Blake and his jazz orchestra, and the dancing Nicholas Brothers, Fayard and Harold. *Pie Pie Blackbird* was made by Vitaphone (a subsidiary of the Hollywood studio Warner Bros.), and for the first time on screen Nina Mae conforms to the Hollywood stereotype of the African American woman as a bandanna-wearing "mammy", confined to the kitchen. The young Nicholas Brothers peer over her shoulder and ask her what she is baking. She tells them it's a blackbird pie. "A blackbird pie!" the brothers exclaim. "There's no such thing as a blackbird pie," remarks a sceptical Fayard. Nina assures the boys, in song, that "It takes a blackbird to make the sweetest sort of pie." Then the camera cuts to a close-up of the blackbird pie as it begins to peel open, and out of it rises Eubie Blake and his orchestra. They play "Memories of You". Nina Mae is transported from the kitchen and into this sequence. Sitting on top of Eubie's piano, she has lost the bandanna, and her mammy attire, and looks every inch the glamorous movie star that she is, wearing a long black dress, and dangling earrings. She sings "Everything I've Got Belongs to You" straight to camera, and includes a scat-singing chorus in the growling vocal style of the jazz innovators Louis Armstrong and Adelaide Hall. The short film continues with more music from Eubie Blake's orchestra, and dancing from the brothers. The *Motion Picture Herald* (June 25, 1932) described the film as "Fairly entertaining, moderately enjoyable if the patron likes the negro band, with its own peculiar type of melody, and the singing negress, Nina Mae McKinney, with her crooning but quite melodious voice." *Film Daily* (June 11, 1932) praised Nina for singing "typical song numbers with a lot of class, and she is a good looker too. She is ably assisted by a typical colored band, who know their harmonizing, both individually and collectively."

In 1936, the director Roy Mack reunited Nina Mae and the Nicholas Brothers for another Vitaphone musical short *The Black Network*. This time Nina Mae had some acting to do as one of the stars of a radio show sponsored by the "Shoe Polish Company". Mezzanine Johnson (Amanda Randolph), the wife of the owner of the company, objects to Nina Mae being the star of the radio show, and insists on performing a number herself. Nina Mae has one number to sing, the soulful 'Half of me wants to be good' by Cliff Hess. The lyrics have Nina Mae recalling her role as Chick in *Hallelujah*, a young black woman torn between good and evil. She sings about being bad and "going to Harlem" and being good and saying "no, tain't right" (to go to Harlem): "One minute I'm singing *Hallelujah/*The next I'm singing let's go to town." Later the clever Nicholas Brothers sing "Lucky Numbers" and perform a dazzling tap routine. The handsome crooner Babe Wallace is Nina Mae's leading man and sings a couple of numbers while the comedy actress Amanda Randolph provides lighter moments as the overbearing Mezzanine Johnson. There is also an energetic number performed by the Washboard Serenaders.

When *Film Daily* (April 1, 1936) reviewed *The Black Network*, it praised the work of its stars: "A troupe of coloured stars, headed by Nina Mae McKinney and the Nicholas Brothers, turn in highly entertaining performances in an unoriginal story of a colored radio sponsor with an ambitious wife who wants to be the whole show. Already familiar to picture audiences, the Nicholas Brothers once more put on a dance routine that always clicks and Nina Mae McKinney sings in the new fashion of "swing." Although the supporting cast is of smaller reputation, each member is effective, particularly three boys [The Washboard Serenaders] who supply music with a washboard, manipulated with thimbles, and an assortment of pots and pans."

When Stephen Bourne interviewed the Nicholas Brothers in London in 1990 he asked them about Nina Mae. They remembered her as a beautiful young star who failed to live up to her early promise because of the lack of roles. The older brother, Fayard, confessed to being star struck: "I'm a big fan of the movies." He felt that, if Hollywood had treated her right, Nina Mae could have had a film career that was comparable to her white contemporaries, Jean Harlow and Carole Lombard: "She had the talent. She could act, sing, dance and wisecrack with the best of them, but she came along too early and there was no place for her."

Nina Mae returned to New York — and the Broadway stage — as one of the stars of the revue *Ballyhoo of 1932* which opened at the 44th Street Theatre on September 6, 1932 and ran for ninety-two performances until

November 26, 1932. The cast also included comedian Bob Hope and, with lyrics by E. Y. "Yip" Harburg, Nina Mae sang "Love, Nuts and Noodles."

Nina Mae's film career may have faltered after *Hallelujah*, but in 1932 she remained popular with African Americans. In March 1932 the black newspaper *The Pittsburgh Courier* asked its readers to name its favourite stars. Nina Mae and Richard B. Harrison, the lead actor in the play *The Green Pastures*, were placed second. Adelaide Hall and Stepin' Fetchit were given third place, and in first place were Ethel Waters and the singing quartet The Mills Brothers.

NOTES ON *HALLELUJAH*

Hallelujah has remained a curiosity for film enthusiasts for over seventy years. For some it represents African American "art", partly because of its association with the Harlem Renaissance, but mostly because of its technical innovations and location filming, especially the emotional mass baptism at the riverside. For example, in 1952 the Cinematheque Belgique survey awarded it 8th position in their "Ten Best Films" list (Sergei Eisenstein's *Battleship Potemkin* was given 1st place). In the Cinematheque Belgique director's ten best lists, two Italian film-makers rated the film highly: Vittorio De Sica placed the film at 9th position, and Luchino Visconti placed it 5th after *La Grande Illusion*; *Greed*; and two by Eisenstein: *Battleship Potemkin*; and *Que Viva Mexico*.

On December 30, 2008, the National Film Preservation Board (NFPB) selected *Hallelujah* for one of its 2008 awards, thus adding the film to the National Film Registry. The twenty-three other titles selected in 2008 included John Boorman's *Deliverance*, Richard Brooks's *In Cold Blood*, Nicholas Ray's *Johnny Guitar*, John Huston's *The Asphalt Jungle*, James Whale's *The Invisible Man*, Sidney Lumet's *The Pawnbroker* and James Cameron's *The Terminator*. Launched in 1989, other films honoured by the NFPB featuring important roles for African American women include *Gone with the Wind* with Hattie McDaniel (selected in 1989); *Carmen Jones* with Dorothy Dandridge (selected in 1992); *Stormy Weather* with Lena Horne (selected in 2001); *Baby Face* with Theresa Harris, *Imitation of Life* with Louise Beavers and Fredi Washington, and *A Raisin in the Sun* with Claudia McNeil, Ruby Dee and Diana Sands (all selected in 2005), and *St Louis Blues* with Bessie Smith (selected in 2006).

CHAPTER 3

THE
BLACK GARBO
1933-1937

FOLLOWING HER TRIP TO PARIS, IN FEBRUARY 1933 NINA Mae crossed the English channel and arrived in London to open (on February 13) in *Chocolate and Cream*, a revue at the Leicester Square Theatre. On February 12 she was interviewed by "J. B." in the *Sunday Dispatch* in "Meet Nina of Harlem! — Amber Girl with the Dancing Feet":

> "It sounds as Scotch as MacDougall but the name belongs to the little coloured girl from South California [sic] who has arrived in London to show us some of the newest hot dances. "I have been acting and dancing and singing all my life," she told me, and it's a pity that cold newsprint cannot convey the harsh, sweet drawl of her voice. There are dozens of shades of Negro skin. Nina is a brown skin, she explains, not high yellow, as some people think. "High yellow is almost white." There is a shadow of contempt in her voice. She spoke of the difficulties that coloured folk occasionally meet with in New York. "Sometimes I've gone into a restaurant, and they say they're full up. But I can see empty tables. It makes you feel" — both hands touched her heart — "awful bad." A funny hat was perched high and straight on her hair. "Please take your hat off," I said. "Oh, I look terrible," she protested. But she looked beautiful. Her hair is not kinky. It is straight and wiry, curling at the ends. She ran her fingers through it, and it stood out, a dark hale for her face. She plays tennis, reads a little, and, laughing very low and sweetly, admitted that she was "in love a little." Her "Good-bye" with the sing-song intonation to which the films have accustomed us, was more than a goodbye. It was a benediction."

Chocolate and Cream had a part-black, part-white cast. Her accompanist, Garland Wilson, later recalled that he did not travel with Nina Mae, but he had joined her at the theatre at least by February 27. Nina Mae and Garland were still appearing in *Chocolate and Cream* in April 1933 when Nina Mae accepted an offer from Britain's leading impresario Charles B. Cochran to star at the Trocadero Restaurant in his revue *Revels in Rhythm*. Cochran, a theatre producer *par excellence* who was known as "Britain's Florenz Ziegfeld", had already transformed the African American stage star Florence Mills into a major figure on London's West End stage in the 1920s. Nina Mae's appearance in *Chocolate and Cream* established her with the general public, while *Revels in Rhythm* exposed her to the rich and elite of London's high society. A Pathé newsreel captured Nina Mae on stage at the Trocadero in *Revels in Rhythm* in an item entitled *London's Famous Clubs and Cabarets. Charles B. Cochran's 'Revels in Rhythm' at the Trocadero Resturarant, London.* It is dated May 15, 1933. An intertitle reads: "London after dark and Mr. Cochran's young ladies are 'stepping out' in style to Annette Mills' melodies." Mills was the older sister of the actor John. She later contributed songs to a BBC radio show called *Molasses Club* (1936) which had an all-black cast, so presumably Mills wrote the music and lyrics of Nina Mae's song "Bring Back the Charleston". Nina Mae is introduced on another intertitle as "the famous West End star" and is seen on stage with Cochran's "young ladies" in long shot, with the audience our front. *The Stage* (June 15, 1933) noted that at the Leicester Square Theatre Nina Mae had added the new torch song "Stormy Weather" to her repertoire. Earlier in the year, this had been written by Harold Arlen and Ted Koehler for Ethel Waters to sing at the Cotton Club.

When Nina Mae arrived in London in 1933, she found herself part of an elite group of black, mostly African American, singers, musicians, and entertainers who were popular with British audiences. They appealed to all classes. One week they could be engaged at a swanky nightclub in London's West End, entertaining the rich and famous, the next at a popular music hall (vaudeville) venue like the Hackney Empire, where they would entertain the working-classes. Nina Mae found herself one of the most popular black artistes in Britain in 1933; others included Paul Robeson, the singer-pianist Leslie 'Hutch' Hutchinson (from Grenada), and the African American duo Layton and Johnstone. Music hall players included the comedy double act Scott and Whaley. It is hardly surprising that the historian Jeffrey Green suggests in his essay "The Negro Renaissance in England", published in *Black Music in the Harlem Renaissance — A Collection of Essays* (1990), that a "Harlem Renaissance" took place in Britain after the economic crash of 1929: "The occurrence of a Harlem Renaissance in England seems unlikely, if not absurd, but New York did not have sole possession of the ideals that led to the black artistic outflow of the Renaissance."

Some blacks who worked in Britain between the two world wars received not only acclaim and popularity but positions in high society. The association of black entertainers with Britain's upper classes and royalty can, in fact, be traced back to the Victorian era. In 1903 the cast of *In Dahomey*, led by Bert Williams and George Walker, were invited to perform for King Edward VII at Buckingham Palace. Jeffrey Green, in "High Society and Black Entertainers in the 1920s and 1930s", published in the journal *New Community* (1987), said: "they mixed with people of rank, wealth, title, and influence. Such contacts suggest a level of social acceptance and thus a British society where some members of the upper classes had liberal views on race relations. Investigation shows that to be a superficial view, however, for black entertainers were seldom truly accepted as individuals, but in general only as symbols. This led to a paradox, since the association of black people with the aristocratic and ruling elite of Britain was seen in America as a social triumph, and was reported as such in the press, biographies, and autobiographies. The reality was that black access to high society was as volatile as show business, and friends were as fickle as audiences."

Nina Mae's association with Charles B. Cochran may have continued if she hadn't upset their relationship. This opened the door for another African American singer. In the summer of 1933, Elisabeth Welch arrived in London to star in *Dark Doings*, a black cast revue which followed *Chocolate and Cream* into the Leicester Square Theatre. Elisabeth's real reason for being in London was an offer from the famous American composer Cole Porter to play a featured role in his forthcoming West End musical *Nymph Errant* starring Gertrude Lawrence. Cochran was the show's producer, and he was wary of Elisabeth, as she explained to Anthony Slide in an interview in *Films in Review* (1987): "He called me to his office in New Bond Street and within minutes he asked if I knew Nina Mae McKinney, another coloured artist who'd been successful in his famous revues at the Trocadero. He spoke with amusement of some of her flare-ups. She thought that to be a star you must be temperamental and nasty. Cochran said he gave her money to bury her father at least four times and her mother twice. I realised he was wondering what I'd be like. He thought he was getting another demon like Nina. However, he soon realised I was nothing like her, and changed the subject. He then talked about the late Florence Mills who took London by storm in *Dover Street to Dixie*, his show of the early 1920s. He adored her. The interview over, we shook hands and I knew I was going to like working for him."

Nina Mae's short career in British films continued with a low-budget comedy called *Kentucky Minstrels* (1934), starring Scott and Whaley, the African American stars of the British variety stage and radio. They had arrived in Britain in 1909, and never returned to the United States. Nina Mae made a guest appearance in the finale with Debroy Somers and his band, who put on blackface for the occasion. *Film Weekly* (May 24, 1934) noted: "As the star of the final spectacular revue, [she] is the best thing in the picture." *Film Weekly* was right. This poor vehicle for Scott and Whaley only came alive when Nina Mae made her 'guest' appearance at the end and sings "I'm in Love With the Band". She looks stunning, and the song is one of the best she sang in the movies. She looks relaxed, and has fun with the number, gyrating and smiling happily when the band plays. An incomplete copy of the film exists in Britain's National Film and Television Archive. It is the finale, with Nina Mae, that is missing. However, through a private collector in the United States, the missing finale has been acquired by the Archive, on videotape. The picture and sound quality is poor. It had been released in America as a short film called *Minstrel Days* and features Scott and Whaley's minstrel act, Nina Mae's song and a fabulous, energetic dance routine by a popular black British music hall troupe of the 1930s called the Eight Black Streaks.

In *Sanders of the River* (1935) she was finally given a starring role (see Chapter 4). That same year (1935), in *BBC — The Voice of Britain*, she was included in a cast that also boasted the literary giants H. G. Wells and George Bernard Shaw. Nina Mae sang Ethel Waters's jazz classic "Dinah" during the broadcast of a radio show called *Music Hall*. Accompanied by Garland Wilson, she looked breathtaking in a gorgeous white gown. This was John Grierson and the GPO Film Unit's "official" documentary about the BBC and it was given a theatrical release. An advertisement in *The Times* for July 27 1935 for the Carlton (cinema) featured Charles Boyer and Loretta Young in *Shanghai* and "Henry Hall, Bernard Shaw, Nina Mae McKinney, H. G. Wells in the Official B. B. C. Film."

Nina Mae's appeal to the British public broadened as she undertook several lengthy and successful variety tours. However, she was not the first African American woman to work in British music halls. Several had successful careers in Britain in the late Victorian and Edwardian era, including Belle Davis and Amy Height. From 1933 to 1937 Nina Mae topped the bill in many of the country's popular music halls in variety shows with such notable and crowd-pleasing artistes as Wee Georgie Wood, Randolph Sutton, George Formby, Will Hay, Max Miller, and Vic Oliver. In London she was seen at the Trocadero Cinema (Elephant and Castle), Holborn Empire, Hackney Empire, New Cross Empire, Palladium, Finsbury Park Empire, Shepherd's Bush Empire and Brixton Empress; outside London she was seen in Glasgow, Manchester, Blackpool, Edinburgh, Cardiff, Birmingham, Liverpool, Bournemouth and Portsmouth. At the Belfast Ritz in 1936 she was featured on the bill with Ken 'Snakehips' Johnson and his Jamaican Emperors of Jazz.

Reviews in *The Stage* newspaper from this period confirm Nina Mae's popularity. A review in *The Stage* (May 18, 1933) of her first appearance at the Hackney Empire described her "appealing personality" and commented that "She assuredly justifies her position at the head of the bill by her ability to put a song over in such items as Underneath a Harlem Moon, Black and Blue, Dinah, and Here Lies Love. In each of these her daintiness of talent and manner ensure vast pleasure to the audience." *The Stage* (October 26, 1933) noted that, at a return engagement at the Hackney Empire, she was featuring "Lazybones", "Stormy Weather" and "It Don't Mean a Thing" in her act. Another review in *The Stage* (Aug 2, 1934) described her "The appealing personality of Nina Mae McKinney holds the attention of audiences this week. Her songs included 'Dinah', 'Black and Blue', 'Let's Fall in Love 'and 'Shuffle Off to Buffalo'. They are mostly calculated to display her talents as a humorous singer, though there are one or two items which strike a deeper note. She is very ably seconded by Garland Wilson whose solo pianoforte work is expertly done." When *The Stage* reviewed her appearance at the Manchester New Hippodrome (April 23, 1936), it noted that "Nina Mae McKinney shares the top of the bill with Bubbles Stewart. She sings a number of popular songs pleasingly, and expertly dances her version of Truckin'. Her two pianists, Rudy Smith and Kirby Walker, score with a syncopation of Dinner for One, Please, James."

When she accepted another engagement at the Hackney Empire, *The Stage* (June 4, 1936) noted that Nina Mae, "who is no stranger here, adds to her many friends each time she appears. Her vivid personality is prominent in her act, and she gives apt expression to 'Shootin' High', 'Black and Blue', 'Solitude', and 'We've Got to Have Something Now', and she is not allowed to go till she has made a graceful little speech of thanks."

In 1934 *The Times* noted that from July to August Nina Mae was appearing in a variety show at the Alhambra (London) with the ballet dancers Anton Dolin and Alicia Markova. Later that year *The Times* (October 31) noted her return to the Alhambra in a revue called *Crossing Trafalgar Square* with the comedian Vic Oliver.

Her last recorded appearance in *The Stage* appears in the May 27, 1937 edition when it noted her appearance at the Brixton Empress in *Mrs. O'Hara's Birthday Party*.

Jazz researcher Howard Rye has noted that Nina Mae suffered bouts of illness throughout her British engagements. He recorded that Nina Mae left London to travel to Australia to open at the Melbourne Tivoli in October 1937 "doing three hot songs and two hooch dances (one from *Sanders of the River*)." In November 1937 illness forced her to cancel after starting an engagement at the Sydney Tivoli. Rye reports that Nina Mae was "back in Harlem" in March 1938. There is no record of her returning to Britain after 1937 but, in her short time there, she proved to be one of the brightest and most popular musical attractions of the 1930s.

CHAPTER 4

SANDERS OF THE RIVER

1935

WHEN BRITAIN'S TOP FILM PRODUCER ALEXANDER KORDA began planning a screen version of Edgar Wallace's novel *Sanders of the River*, set in British West Africa, Wallace hoped that the role of his African chief Bosambo would be offered to Charles Laughton. The celebrated actor won a Best Actor Oscar in 1933 for playing Henry VIII for Korda. Until then, no black actor had ever played an important dramatic role in a British film. In 1930 Laughton had played a dark-skinned Italian with great success in Edgar Wallace's thriller *On the Spot* on the London stage. Therefore it seems likely that Wallace's preference for Laughton was a serious one. Laughton was a clever and versatile actor, so why not allow him to play an African in blackface? However, the charismatic Paul Robeson had also made an impact on the London stage as a dramatic star in productions of William Shakespeare's *Othello* (1930) and Eugene O'Neill's *All God's Chillun' Got Wings* (1933). In America he had made a successful transition to cinema in O'Neill's *The Emperor Jones* (1933). In 1934 Robeson was a more obvious choice for the role of Bosambo, and it was Robeson who Korda signed for the part. The film was directed by Korda's brother Zoltan.

According to one of Robeson's biographers, Marie Seton, in *Paul Robeson*, (1958), the first draft of the screenplay presented his character "with both credibility and dignity and Robeson became engrossed in developing this character…It seemed to him that if he could portray an African chief on the screen with cultural accuracy, then he was making a contribution to the understanding of tribal culture which he considered was a part of his own heritage. The more he had studied Africa, the more strongly he felt that he was essentially an African." However, Robeson's association with Korda was not a happy one. During the editing process extra scenes were added — without Robeson's knowledge — that glorified the British Empire and colonialism. Robeson had every right to be embarrassed by the version that was released to the public, and consequently he disowned the film. He told the *Sunday Worker* (May 10, 1936): "the twist in the picture which was favourable to English imperialism was accomplished during the cutting of the picture after it was filmed. I had no idea that it would have such a turn *after* I had acted in it. Moreover, when it was shown at its premiere in London and I saw what it was, I was called to the stage and in protest refused to perform."

In *Sanders of the River* the paternalistic District Commissioner Sanders (Leslie Banks) refers to the local African community as his "black children". Robeson's first appearance in the film is shocking. Naked, except for a leopard skin covering his private parts, he stoops and humbly addresses

Sanders as his "lord and master." It is in this sequence that we learn about Bosambo. He is a Liberian convict and a prison escapee. In spite of this, he wins the trust of Sanders, who elevates him to leader of a village, an appointment which gains him respectability. Enter Nina Mae as Lilongo, who has been taken prisoner by the evil King Mofolaba, whose life's ambition is to make a drum out of Bosambo's skin. Lilongo is rescued by Bosambo and they fall in love, marry and have two children. In *Best of British Cinema and Society 1930-1970* (1983), Jeffrey Richards says that "Bosambo is conceived entirely in Western terms as an archetype well established in imperial fiction: a combination of doglike devotion, boastful sexuality and childish naughtiness. Similarly, his relationship with his wife Lilongo is seen in strictly European terms. They love each other. She bosses him about. He risks his life to rescue her. There is little appreciation of the African character judged in African terms."

When Robeson filmed *Sanders* he befriended some of the African extras on the set, but he was unprepared for their reaction to him. The actress Flora Robson later recalled in the British (BBC) television documentary *Paul Robeson* (1978): "he wore a leopard skin and he was ticked off by a Prince of the Ashanti who was up at Oxford and said 'What do you wear a leopard skin for?' So Paul said 'Well, what do *you* wear in Africa? Tweeds?' And the Prince said 'Yes, We do.' They didn't like him. They thought as an educated man he shouldn't play these primitive parts."

The contact Robeson made with Africans on the set of *Sanders*, and some of his other British films (*Song of Freedom, King Solomon's Mines*), had a lasting impact on him, as his son, Paul Robeson, Jr, later explained in the British (Channel 4) television documentary *Songs of Freedom — Paul Robeson and the Black American Struggle* (1986): "During his film career he met many Africans on the set of films like *Sanders of the River*. Among the extras of *Sanders* was Jomo Kenyatta, the famous burning spear, who then became the first President of Kenya. So culturally he was drawn to the Africans on the set. He found his own African roots, you might say, and became radicalised by the African anti-colonial fighters of that time like Jomo Kenyatta."

Sanders of the River was met with a hostile reception from black critics. In 1937 the Nigerian scholar Dr Nnamdi Azikiwe complained in his book *Renascent Africa* about the film's "exaggeration of African mentality. I feel that what is being paraded in the world today as art or literature is nothing short of propaganda." Robeson was singled out by his most outspoken black critic, Marcus Garvey, the Jamaican nationalist leader who is credited with inspiring black consciousness on an international scale. In the 1930s, while basing himself in London, Garvey denounced Robeson's films. In 1935, in the American journal *Black Man*, Garvey condemned Robeson's stage and screen image: "Paul Robeson cannot see that he is being used to the dishonour and discredit of his race…Robeson is pleasing England by the gross slander and libel of the Negro."

Nina Mae may have been spared the anger of Marcus Garvey, but contemporary white film critics were not impressed with her performance in *Sanders*. They were unanimous that Korda has miscast her. *The Cinema* (April 3, 1935) charged that she "strikes a jarring note as neither her appearance nor her American accent is conducive to conviction." *Kinematograph Weekly* (April 4, 1935) was a little kinder, saying that she was "a trifle reminiscent of a Harlem cabaret star, but she, nevertheless, acquits herself well." The *Birmingham Post* (April 11, 1935) praised Nina Mae for her work in *Hallelujah* but complained that she was too sophisticated for the role of Lilongo, and came across as a displaced cabaret artiste from New York's Harlem. *Film Weekly* (April 12, 1935) was harsher: "Miss McKinney is just about as much at home in the jungle as, say, a Harlem night-club entertainer. Sophistication is written all over her personality, and her accent is redolent of chewing-gum." James Agate in *The Tatler* (April 17, 1935) found that both Nina Mae and Robeson were "too lady-like and gentlemanly for the roles." Dr Nnamdi Azikwe asked: "Why did Mr. Paul Robeson choose to play such an ignominious role to undervalue African mentality? A man of his education seems to be an enigma to me. As for Miss McKinney, the less said about her the better. Her education is not comparable to that of Robeson."

In 1989 Martin Bauml Duberman, another of Robeson's many biographers, commented in *Paul Robeson* that Nina Mae was "woefully miscast in *Sanders* — that is, if one assumes the Kordas had ever intended portraying an African woman rather than a commercialized Harlem transplant. Light-skinned, Occidental in features and mannerisms, eyebrows plucked, the sleek, glamorous, American-accented McKinney was disastrously wrong in the role of Bosambo's native wife." And yet, who else could have played the part? There were no African leading ladies in 1935, and the only major black female stars available were American. If not Nina Mae, then Josephine Baker? Or Ethel Waters? Or Adelaide Hall? In 1938 Hall did, in fact, play a similar role in *The Sun Never Sets*, a London stage play based on Wallace's *Sanders* stories. Nina Mae was the only choice for the movie role.

Contemporary reviews of Nina Mae's portrayal of Lilongo were harsh but, half a century later, in 1988, Donald Bogle took the trouble to reassess her performance in *Blacks in American Films and Television — An Illustrated Encyclopedia*: "As an African princess she was a glitzy Hollywoodized creation, her voice — with its sweet suggestion of a southern accent — totally inappropriate, her makeup and costumes overdone. Yet the movie itself was so fake and trumped up that her highly glamorous presence was one of the few amusing offbeat bright spots."

There have also been attempts to reassess her most memorable sequence in the film. Lilongo is required to sing a lullaby to her two children. In *Africa on Film — Beyond Black and White* (1994), Kenneth M. Cameron describes the scene as "remarkable" and the director's "mostly visual riposte to his brother's pro-white, pro-British drum-beating." He adds: "The song may be un-African, but the sequence is a moving one whose dramatization of the love of a black woman for a black child obliterated the "savage" stereotype. It also extended the inner life of Bosambo in a way that most previous films had not allowed African characters... it gave him an emotional and social life and marked a rare archetype, one that was both African and female, the Black Wife." Cameron also pointed out that "The Black Wife" portrayed in the British films of Paul Robeson: Lilongo in *Sanders*; Ruth Zinga (Elisabeth Welch) in *Song of Freedom* (1936); and Gara (Princess Kouka) in *Jericho* (1937), "was not a vamp; to the contrary, especially as embodied by Elizabeth (sic) Welch in *Song of Freedom*, she was a warm, comforting, supporting woman of great personal courage. Empowerment came through her husband; expression of self was also made through his desires, especially the return to Africa. Yet she stands out in British African films of this period because she was a woman who was a central character; so was Bosambo's wife in *Sanders* (Nina Mae McKinney). And they stand out because the Robeson characters *did* have wives."

In 2001 Sheila Tully Boyle and Andrew Bunie endorsed Cameron's view in *Paul Robeson — The Years of Promise and Achievement*: "The wonderful scene in *Sanders* when Nina Mae McKinney sings the lullaby "Little Black Dove" to her child was another first. Showing a black mother's feelings of love and tenderness for her child and suggesting by extension an emotional life for her husband as well was an image hitherto denied blacks on the screen."

Though neither child was credited on the cast list, Bosambo and Lilongo's children were played by Anthony Papafio and Deara Williams. Papafio was born in London, the son of a West African seaman who occasionally worked as a film extra. Deara Williams born in Butetown, Cardiff in south Wales to an African father and his African-Welsh wife.

Sanders of the River proved to be one of Robeson's most commercially successful films, in spite of his public condemnation of it. In fact it was so successful when first shown in 1935 that it was reissued in 1938, 1943 and 1947. Robeson's recording of the "Canoe Song" was a hit and the box office success of *Sanders* encouraged Alexander Korda to produce more jingoistic films that glorified the British Empire, including *The Drum* (1938), set in India, and *The Four Feathers* (1939), set in the Sudan.

Paul Robeson made a big impact on the British public in *Sanders*. In a letter to Stephen Bourne, published in his book *Black in the British Frame* (2001), Mrs Marjorie Bryan wrote: "We saw the same Paul Robeson films over and over again. *Sanders of the River* was my favourite. He appeared at a time when there were very few black actors. He was a commanding figure. He stood out, and was noticed. The people in the north of England are a loyal lot and they were sad when Paul Robeson was in trouble. They signed petitions. People in England didn't forget him."

Nina Mae was scheduled to co-star with Robeson again in his next British film, *Song of Freedom* (1936), but the role was given to Elisabeth Welch. This may have had something to do with Nina Mae's affair with Robeson while they were filming *Sanders*. According to Martin Bauml Duberman, the "brief" love affair was well enough known to reach Robeson's mother-in-law, Ma Goode, in America. Ma Goode informed her daughter, Eslanda, who already knew. Apparently Nina Mae had described Paul as "her man": "Essie wrote back to her mother [in a letter dated January 20, 1935], and added an elaborate, unconvincing anecdote about how she had decoyed Paul away from seeing McKinney off at the boat train by getting her hair and nails done and putting on a dazzling new outfit for a cocktail party at the Kordas', where she was "an immediate success," was asked out to dinner by Robert Donat, and so excited Paul's attention that he took her out for dinner himself instead of going to see McKinney off."

CHAPTER 5

TELEVISION PIONEER

1937

SHORTLY AFTER HER ARRIVAL IN BRITAIN, NINA MAE WAS invited to participate in one of John Logie Baird's experimental television programmes. Logie Baird was a television pioneer who was transmitting programmes live from his studio at 16 Portland Place in London. On February 17, 1933 Nina Mae made history when she became the first black artiste to be seen on television, albeit an experimental programme. Nina Mae's appearance was announced in *The Times* for 11 to 11.30pm: "Television transmission by the Baird process (Vision): Nina Mae McKinney (song and dance)." *The Times* also advertised Nina Mae's first appearance on BBC radio on May 10, 1933. On October 4, 1933 Josephine Baker, on a rare trip to London from her home in France, followed Nina Mae into Logie Baird's studio for another experimental transmission.

Three years later, on November 2, 1936, the British Broadcasting Corporation (BBC) launched its regular, high-definition television service at Alexandra Palace (also known as "Ally Pally") which was situated in a suburb ten miles from the centre of London. Following opening speeches, a variety programme commenced at 3.23 p. m. with the musical-comedy star Adele Dixon singing "Television". This was followed by an appearance by the talented African American double act, Buck and Bubbles, then starring in London's West End in the revue *Transatlantic Rhythm*. The BBC's listings magazine *Radio Times* described Buck and Bubbles as "a coloured pair who are versatile comedians who dance, play the piano, sing and cross-chat'. However, there were no more than about four hundred television sets in use for the opening ceremony. Since they could cost as much as £100 each, they were an expensive commodity. So, on November 2, 1936, television viewing was very much a minority interest. In addition, transmissions covered the London area only, a radius of about twenty-five miles from Alexandra Palace.

In the pre-war years of BBC television (1936-39), before the outbreak of the Second World War on September 3, 1939 interrupted the service, black entertainers continued to make an important contribution to BBC music and variety programmes. Said Bruce Norman in *Here's Looking at You — The Story of British Television 1908-39* (1984): "In the first years at Alexandra Palace the programme emphasis, if there *was* an emphasis, was on entertainment." Norman then quotes Cecil Madden, one of BBC television's earliest and most important producers: "We had such frightfully good entertainment available to us. There were shows going on in all the London nightclubs and a great deal of money was being spent. There was a cabaret, an artist or two in every place — Quaglino's, the Windmill, the Ritz — everywhere. Of very high class. The sort of people we really wanted and so we were able to draw on a great deal of ready-made entertainment without having to do an awful lot of rehearsing ourselves."

Nina Mae was among the "very high class" entertainers who attracted the attention of the BBC, and three months after the television service was launched, she was one of the first artistes to be given her own variety show. *Ebony* was transmitted live from Alexandra Palace on Saturday February 27, 1937 and featured Nina Mae and the African American tap dancer Johnny Nit (who had arrived in London in the 1920s with one of Lew Leslie's *Blackbirds* revues). The BBC Television Orchestra was also featured and the presentation was by Dallas Bower. In the programme log that has survived in the BBC's Written Archive, Nina Mae sang three songs: "Papa Tree Top Tall", "Harlem Moon" and "Why Am I So Black and Blue?" She is accompanied by two black pianists: Kirby Walker and Rudy Smith. The BBC's listings magazine *Radio Times* (February 19, 1937) published a full-page portrait of Nina Mae, taken by the London photographer 'Cannons of Hollywood', in its television supplement. *Ebony* was transmitted from 9.40-10.00pm in an evening of programmes that also included a dramatic sketch entitled *The Underground Murder Mystery*, a comedy sketch entitled *Catching the Male*, a gardening programme, and the newsreel British Movietone News.

In a second show, *Dark Laughter*, transmitted on Saturday June 5, 1937, Nina Mae was featured with the Jamaican trumpet player Leslie Thompson. The production was by Dallas Bower. Accompanied by two black pianists, Kirby Walker and Yorke de Sousa, Nina Mae sang "Copper Coloured Gal of Mine" and "Big Boy Blue". The *Radio Times* acknowledged Nina Mae's second show with a photograph from *Ebony* featuring Nina Mae with Kirby Walker and Rudy Smith.

Ebony, Dark Laughter and some of the other pre-war television shows were influenced by the black Broadway musicals and revues of the Harlem Renaissance, as well as revues from New York's famous nightclubs, such as the Cotton Club. Throughout the 1920s and 1930s some of these shows had been transplanted to London's West End. In addition to Nina Mae, several other African American entertainers who had relocated to London found themselves showcased in the new medium of television. These included Eunice Wilson and Garland Wilson (*Burnt Sepia*, 1937), Valaida (*Dark Highlights*, 1938) and Adelaide Hall (*Harlem in Mayfair* and *Dark Sophistication*, both 1939). Other African Americans who were featured in pre-war television programmes included Fats Waller, Alberta Hunter, Elisabeth Welch, The Mills Brothers and Paul Robeson.

When the pioneer television producer Cecil Madden was interviewed in the *Radio Times* in 1981, he explained how he found artists for some of these early music and variety shows: "There were nightclubs everywhere, and marvellous American artists coming over to appear in them. We would get them all up to Ally Pally for a £25 fee — Sophie Tucker was the only one who ever got more, on the grounds that she had to bring her own accompanist. We paid £40 for the two of them."

In an interview with Stephen Bourne, published in *Black and White in Colour — Black People in British Television Since 1936* (1992), Nina Mae's contemporary Elisabeth Welch remembered what it was like to work in pre-war television at Alexandra Palace: "You had to climb over a whole sea of cables just to get to the camera, which never moved. You just stood there, in front of it, and sang your song. It was static, nerve-wracking, but amusing. Everything was live. If you made a mistake, you couldn't just re-do it from scratch."

In 1937, when Nina Mae's television shows were transmitted live, no technology existed to record them. However, she was invited to take part in the BBC's *Television Demonstration Film* (1937), produced and directed by Dallas Bower, who had worked with her on *Ebony* and *Dark Laughter*. It is one of the few surviving records of pre-war television. *Television Demonstration Film* is a film survey of BBC television programmes during the first six months of operation (November 1936 to May 1937), intended for manufacturers and retailers to show sample types of programmes transmitted. The announcer Leslie Mitchell stresses that this is a film and television is always transmitted live. A rich variety of artistes were filmed, including Sidonie Goossens, who plays the harp; Margot Fonteyn, who dances a ballet solo; Irene Prador, who sings "Tales from the Vienna Woods". Nina Mae sings "Papa Tree Top Tall". A contract addressed to Nina Mae has survived in the BBC's Written Archive. It records that she filmed her sequence on April 9, 1937 at the Stoll Film Studio in Cricklewood (North West London) and she was paid twenty guineas (£21) "including the services of own two pianists". Her address is given as C/O Messrs. B. Montague, Ltd., 60-66 Wardour Street, London W1.

Since 1937 Nina Mae's appearance in the *Television Demonstration Film* has been seen in just about every documentary made about the history of British television. These include *Salute to A. P.* (BBC, 1954), *This Was the Future* (BBC, 1957), *The Birth of Television* (BBC, 1977), *Magic Rays of Light* (BBC, 1981), *That's Television Entertainment* (1986) and *The A to Z of TV* (Channel 4, 1990).

CHAPTER 6

"RACE MOVIES"

1938-1939

ON HER RETURN TO THE UNITED STATES, NINA MAE starred in three films known as "race movies". These were made independently outside Hollywood, usually by white producers and directors, and featuring blacks casts. These low-budget productions resembled Hollywood "B" pictures (films made on small budgets and then screened as "support" features to the main attraction). "Race movies" were made almost exclusively for African American audiences and were rarely, if ever, distributed abroad. Occasionally a "foreign" film starring an expatriate like Paul Robeson or Josephine Baker was exported to the United States and packaged for black cinema audiences as a "race movie." During the years of America's Depression, black audiences sought temporary refuge from their troubles in racially segregated cinemas which showed "race movies". Black audiences were provided with images denied to them in Hollywood films at that time, including black gangsters and cowboys. There were also numerous cabaret sequences. Though she only starred in three "race movies" in a short time frame (1938-39), Nina Mae emerged as one of the most popular stars of the genre. This was mostly due to her fame and popularity with the African American public.

Some criticism was aimed at the "race movies", especially those directed by the African American Oscar Micheaux, for casting only "light-skinned" black actors as the heroes and heroines. Darker skinned actors were cast as either villains or stereotypical buffoons. However, for many African Americans, the "race movies" of the 1920s, 1930s and 1940s provided them with their only alternative to Hollywood. Interviewed in G. William Jones's *Black Cinema Treasures — Lost and Found* (1991), Harrel Gordon Tillman, a former actor in "race movies", commented: "That was precisely the charm of those films...with the Francine Everetts and the Nina Mae McKinneys in them. I don't care how black you were or how fair you were — you could see someone in those films that looked like you...I could see somebody who looked like me. I could see somebody who looked like my brother. You could see those things and you could see yourself in those films."

Nina Mae starred in three "race movies" but there should have been a fourth. In February 1938 Nina Mae was in Australia and due to return to the United States to star opposite the actor-dancer Ralph Cooper in a musical called *The Duke is Tops*. In 1937 Cooper had joined forces with the white Harry Popkin to become a partner in Million Dollar productions, a company that had been set up to produce low-budget films for black audiences. With the financial backing of Popkin, Cooper wrote, directed and starred in *Bargain with Bullets* (1937), and it proved to be a great success. In *The Duke is Tops*, Nina Mae would play Ethel, a beautiful young singer who is offered a chance to star in a Broadway show. Nina Mae, who was known as the "Black Garbo", was the perfect choice to play Cooper's leading lady, as he was known as the "Dark Gable". However, Nina Mae fell ill in Australia, and had to be replaced. An up-and-coming young singer called Lena Horne was offered the role. Later that year, after her return from Australia, Nina Mae made her "race movie" debut with a terrific performance in a melodrama with songs called *Gang Smashers* (1938).

Gang Smashers (1938) began life as *Gun Moll* and, as a testament to her star status, Nina Mae was billed solo over the title. She played Laura Jackson, an undercover agent who works as a cabaret entertainer for the gang leader Gat Dalton (J. Lawrence Criner). Dalton runs the corrupt "Harlem Protective Association" and is madly infatuated with Laura, the main attraction at his nightclub. In reality Laura is a clever detective, sent by the police department to spy on Dalton, and help bring him to justice. When Gat learns of the deception of another undercover detective, Lefty Wilson (Monte Hawley), his gang takes him for a "ride." With the assistance of Laura, the police successfully trail the kidnapper's car. In an exciting climax Lefty fights Gat, and subdues him. At the end, Lefty and Laura declare their love for each other.

Gang Smashers is easily Nina Mae's best "race movie". Though made on a low-budget, the film is as good as any of the crime dramas being produced in Hollywood by Warner Bros., and Nina Mae gives a *tour-de-force* as the beautiful, glamorous and brave undercover detective who doubles as a cabaret star. A major flaw in the film is the performance of comedy actor Mantan Moreland. He conforms to the Hollywood stereotype of the bug-eyed buffoon but his antics are embarrassing. In the cabaret sequences in Gat's nightclub, Nina Mae excels. In the first sequence, she sings 'I Just Can't See it Your Way', a torch song. She is accompanied by Phil Moore and his orchestra who are credited on the cast list, and Moore is also credited as the film's musical director. Moore later worked in Hollywood with Lena Horne when she was contracted to M-G-M, and also collaborated with Dorothy Dandridge on her nightclub act. In the second cabaret sequence, Nina Mae conducts the orchestra while Neva Peoples sings a rousing number celebration of Harlem with "That's What You Get in Harlem". Peoples reassures the audience that "Harlem is heaven/'twill always be that way/brown skin feet truckin' down the street/ those Creole babies really lift their feet/sunny smiles that can't be beat/ that's what you get in Harlem."

In a lovely contrast to her previous, melancholy, cabaret appearance in the film, Nina Mae conducts the orchestra with a sense of fun. Lightheartedly she reacts to Neva Peoples' performance by acting silly, pulling faces and jumping up and down. She is a joy to watch, and one can only imagine what her vaudeville act was like.

Throughout *Gang Smashers*, Nina Mae is presented as a glamorous and sophisticated woman of the world who is far removed from the bandanna-wearing mammies of Hollywood. With this role, Nina Mae offered a positive and more realistic alternative to Bette Davis's scatterbrained servant girl Zette, played by the lovely but underrated Theresa Harris, in that year's Southern melodrama *Jezebel* (1938). Regrettably, Nina Mae's two other "race movies" were poor, and wasted her.

The Devil's Daughter (1939) is acknowledged as the first feature to be filmed on location in Jamaica. In this melodramatic tale, a poor script fails to make much sense, or offer its cast much in the way of acting challenges. In spite of its tantalizing title (its working title had been *Pocomania*), there is no devil in the film, and the "daughters" are so blandly written and acted, they could have done with a devil to breathe some life into them! Ida James plays the "good" sister, Sylvia Walton, an American heiress who inherits a plantation in Jamaica. The plantation workers are all unconvincing "Jamaicans" because there is no hint of patois in the way they speak. Sylvia's half-sister is the "bad" Isabelle, played by Nina Mae. She lives on the plantation, and has staked a claim to the property. After refusing Sylvia's generous offer to share it, Isabelle devises a scheme with Phillip (Jack Carter), the plantation overseer, to exploit Sylvia's tendency to believe in superstitions. Phillip convinces the gullible Sylvia that she is going to be sacrificed in an obeah ceremony unless she leaves the island. However, since Isabelle has no idea how to perform obeah, and states that she will not go through with the sacrifice anyway, there is no drama in the story at all.

On the plus side, *The Devil's Daughter* opens with a marvellous sequence of documentary footage that features a group of local Jamaican singers, dancers and musicians. They bring to life the popular Jamaican folk song "Linstead Market". It is pure joy! On the negative side, the comedy actor Hamtree Harrington provides comic relief as Percy Jackson, but his scenes are not funny. For example, in a sub-plot, Percy is tricked into believing that his soul was transferred into a pig so that it wouldn't get stolen by ghosts.

Nina Mae's third and final "race movie" was *Straight to Heaven* (1939), a melodramatic story about syndicate crime in Harlem's black community.

Nina Mae was cast as a former cabaret star called Ida Williams, now happily married with a young son. A parallel story concerned the rise to fame of Nina Mae's son Jimmy, a boy soprano played by Jackie Ward. He was advertised on the film's posters as "the colored Bobby Breen." Breen was a white teenage singing star of Hollywood movies in the late 1930s. *Straight to Heaven* is primarily a vehicle for Jackie Ward, and Nina Mae is used for her name value only (she is billed solo above the title in the film's opening credits). Ward is given three songs, and Nina Mae only one. In the obligatory cabaret sequence, Nina Mae sings an attractive blues number, "When the Dark Becomes Dawn". Its composer, Josef Myrow, hailed from Russia and was later Oscar nominated twice. His most famous composition was "You Make Me Feel So Young", popularized by Frank Sinatra. For the first time on screen, Nina Mae looks tired and weary. It is hardly surprising, considering the poor script. Though only in her late twenties, she looks much older, and the role gives her little to do except emote when her husband goes to prison on a false charge, and her son goes missing. *Straight to Heaven* was Nina Mae's last starring role in a movie and, though top-billed, it is sad to see her relegated to nothing more than a supporting role in a vehicle for the less than talented "Harlem discovery" Jackie Ward. Also in the supporting cast is James Baskette, as "1st Detective". He later won a special Oscar for his role as Uncle Remus in Walt Disney's popular success *Song of the South* (1946). Lorenzo Tucker, the former "black Valentino" of Oscar Micheaux's earlier "race movies", is relegated to a minor supporting role as a villain called "Ace".

When movie roles dried up, Nina Mae returned to the stage. In 1940 she joined the all-black cast of the musical comedy *Tan Manhattan*. It had a score by two prominent African Americans from the world of musical theatre: Eubie Blake (music) and Andy Razaf (lyrics). Nina Mae starred alongside the comedian Flournoy Miller, and the singer/dancer Avon Long. The show opened at the Howard Theatre in Washington on January 24, 1941 and received favorable reviews. Nina Mae was singled out by the critics for her two torch songs: "Say Hello to the Folks Back Home" and "I'll Take a Nickel for a Dime." For a time it looked as if *Tan Manhattan* would return Nina Mae to Broadway for the first time since *Ballyhoo of 1932*, but when the show arrived in New York in February 1941, it only got as far as the Apollo Theatre in Harlem, where it closed after a short run. Nina Mae then toured with the Pancho Diggs Orchestra. In *Swing City — Newark Nightlife, 1925-50* (1991), Barbara J. Kukla explained what happened when Nina Mae joined the Orchestra:

"Beautiful and a natural talent, she was as well an all-round entertainer, gifted with an appealing singing voice and a natural flair for comedy. McKinney also had a "name" that could get the band considerably more work than Diggs could secure on his own. So the band's name was changed to the Nina Mae McKinney Orchestra for a cross-country tour. For Diggs, the deal proved to be a mixed blessing. On the one hand, McKinney's name was a drawing card. Black audiences across America knew and idolized her as a beautiful but wacky screen star on the order of Carole Lombard. In New York she was a favorite at the Apollo Theater, where she teamed with the top male comedians of the day in an act similar to that of the old-time entertainers Butterbeans and Susie. Yet with McKinney fronting the band, its importance musically was greatly obscured. Rather than viewing McKinney as the vocalist, the patrons saw the musicians as the backdrop of her act."

They toured for about a year as Nina Mae McKinney and her Orchestra but all it did for Pancho Diggs's Orchestra was to help it lose its identity. The association ended in 1943 when Diggs was drafted into the Army.

Throughout the 1930s, Nina Mae was linked to her "manager", Jimmy Monroe (James N. Monroe), described in some sources as a "hustler" and a "pimp", but her "marriage" to him has not been confirmed. So far, attempts to locate a marriage certificate have failed, though some sources claim that they were married in 1940 and divorced in 1941. Monroe definitely married the legendary jazz singer Billie Holiday on August 25, 1941 in Elkton, Maryland (see Ken Vail's *Lady Day's Diary — The Life of Billie Holiday 1937-1959*, 1996). Monroe was described in some press reports of the marriage as the "thirty-year-old former husband of Nina Mae McKinney." It was the first marriage for Holiday who explained in her autobiography *Lady Sings the Blues* (1956) that she married Monroe "to prove something to somebody". She was referring to her mother and manager, Joe Glaser, who both warned her about him. Monroe was the younger brother of Clark Monroe, who ran a popular nightclub in Harlem. Holiday described Monroe as a man who had taste and class and was "the most beautiful man I'd laid eyes on since Buck Clayton…Jimmy had been in Europe for quite a while. Over there, especially in England, as the big beautiful husband of a big star [Nina Mae], he had been quite a big deal himself. In London he had hung out with nothing but white women. He had brought at least one big beautiful Cockney chick back to New York with him. He was managing her when I met him." The Monroe/Holiday marriage was doomed from the start, partly because the "Cockney chick" remained "in town" and continued her relationship with Monroe after he had wed Holiday. "I saw the lipstick," she said. As a direct consequence of this discovery Holiday wrote the lyrics to one of her greatest songs: "Don't Explain". Holiday claims she had been with Monroe for a year when she "got wise" to something else about her husband: "Jimmy smoked something strange." Some sources claim that Holiday became addicted to heroin during her marriage to Monroe. In fact, Holiday said that she began using drugs with Monroe to give them something in common and hold their shaky marriage together. A few years later Monroe was sentenced to nine months in prison for smuggling marijuana between Mexico and California. The couple were eventually divorced.

When Jimmy Monroe died on December 31, 1993, at the age of eighty-three, he was quoted in David Hinckley's tribute in *The New York Daily News*: "Before he met Billie Holiday he was married to Nina Mae McKinney, the stunning early dance and movie star who died young. Monroe later said she was one of the most beautiful women he ever saw, but that she always felt uncomfortable with her success."

Nina Mae McKinney.

Nina Mae McKinney and Daniel L. Haynes in Hallelujah *(1929).*

Nina Mae McKinney and Debroy Somers and his band in Kentucky
Minstrels *(1934).*

Nina Mae McKinney in Kentucky Minstrels *(1934).*

Paul Robeson and Nina Mae McKinney in Sanders of the River *(1935).*

Nina Mae McKinney in Sanders of the River *(1935).*

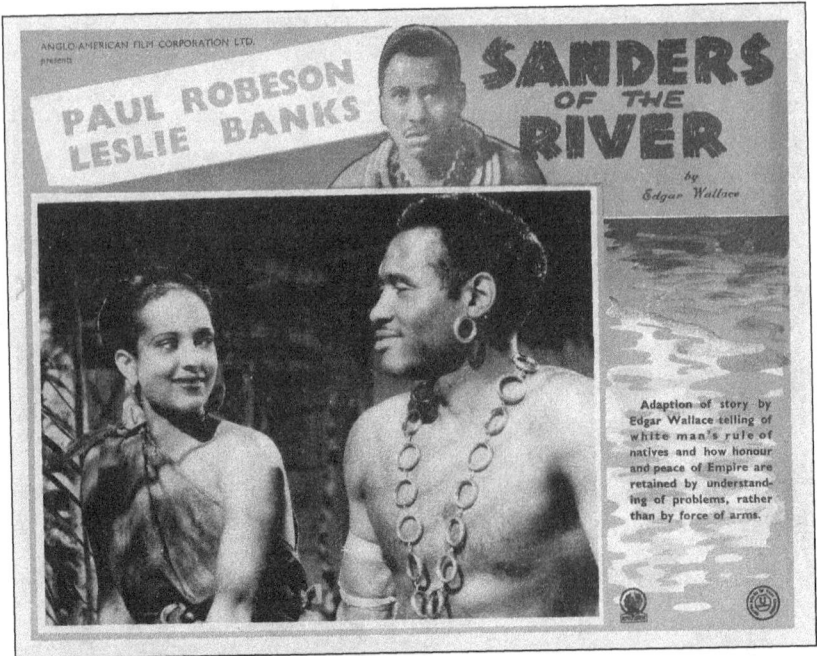

Front of House Still for Sanders of the River *(1935).*

Nina Mae McKinney in Sanders of the River *(1935).*

Nina Mae McKinney.

Nina Mae McKinney.

Jean Harlow, Nina Mae McKinney and Garland Wilson in Reckless *(1935).*

Nina Mae McKinney.

Nina Mae McKinney.

Radio Pictorial *(November 15, 1935).*

Nina Mae McKinney

A great stage personality who will be seen on Saturday

Radio Times *(February 19, 1937).*

Radio Times *(May 28, 1937).*

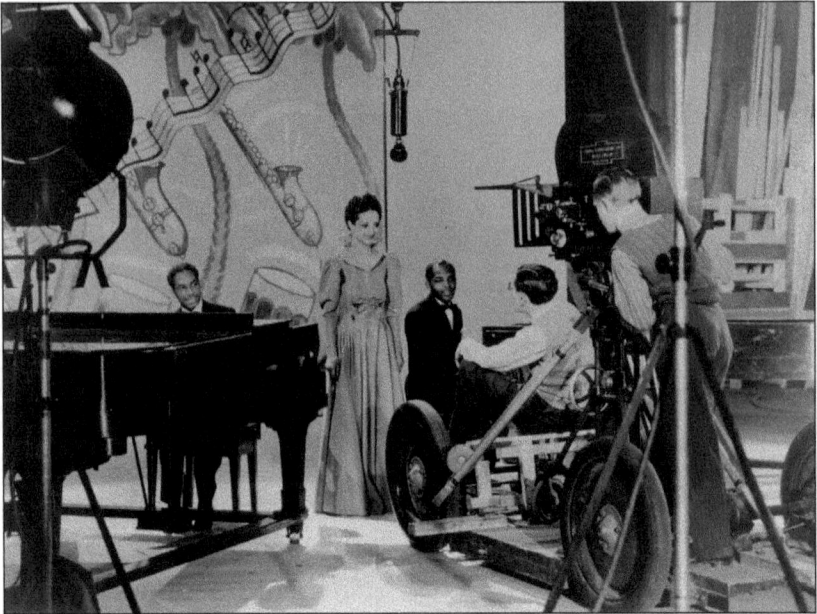

Television Demonstration Film (1937). Nina Mae McKinney with pianist Yorke de Souza on left and director Dallas Bower sitting under the camera.

Nina Mae McKinney in The Devil's Daughter *(1939).*

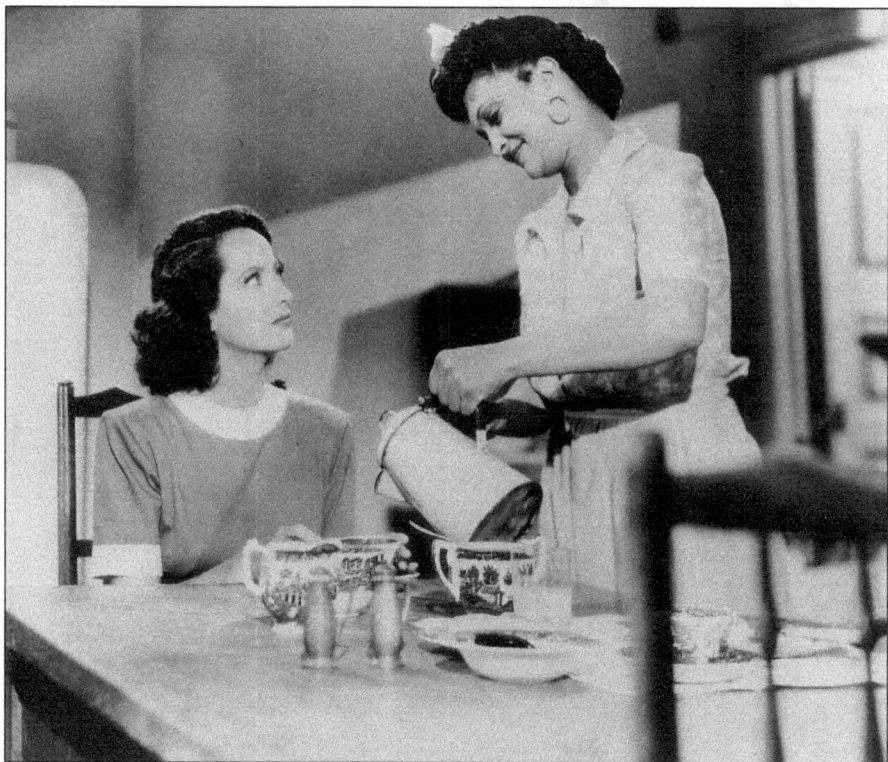

Merle Oberon and Nina Mae McKinney in Dark Waters *(1944).*

In movie "Pinky," Nina berates Jeanne Craine. First Negro woman signed by MGM, her first film was "Hallelujah."

WHAT HAPPENED TO:

NINA MAE MCKINNEY?

Accompanied by McLin in Harlem home, Nina sings "Good For Nothin' Joe."

IN 1950, when actress Nina Mae McKinney completed her role in the movie *Pinky*, she virtually closed the door on her acting and singing career. She virtually retired to Harlem, shunned entertainment floodlights for three years. Today, Nina Mae is preparing a return to show business in a new act with ex-Count Basie guitarist Jimmy McLin, hopes it will return her to stardom.

19

Hue *magazine article (February 1954).*

CHAPTER 7

NINA MAE'S RETURN TO HOLLYWOOD

1944 TO 1950

IN 1944, WHEN NINA MAE RETURNED TO HOLLYWOOD, ten years had almost passed since she had briefly appeared in M-G-M's *Reckless*. However, the situation for African American actresses in the movies had not improved. Hattie McDaniel may have won the Oscar for Best Supporting Actress in 1939 for *Gone with the Wind* but, in spite of this triumph, she could not avoid being cast as loveable, bandanna-wearing mammies.

The 1940 United States census reported that of the 2,426 actors in Los Angeles, only 51 were black. Of the 910 male dancers, showmen, and athletes, a mere 33 were black. Of the 743 actresses working in Hollywood movies, only a paltry 15 were African American. In addition to Hattie McDaniel and her sister Etta, among those women were Butterfly McQueen (famous for playing Scarlett O'Hara's servant Prissy in *Gone with the Wind*), Louise Beavers, Theresa Harris, Jeni Le Gon, and Lillian Yarbo. And yet, there were glimmers of change, especially after the United States entered the Second World War in December 1941.

In 1942, when Lena Horne signed a seven-year contract with M-G-M, it was a breakthrough for black artistes. In 1943 she co-starred with Ethel Waters in *Cabin in the Sky*, the first film to give a black female star (Waters) above-the-title billing. However, Lena, and the Trinidadian pianist and singer Hazel Scott, were the exceptions to the rule. Although they were mostly used as segregated "speciality" acts in musicals, confined to sequences that could be cut out by distributors in the American south who objected, they were always presented as sophisticated and glamorous, as opposed to bandanna-wearing mammies or maids. At that time Southern distributors and censors did not take kindly to African American women like Lena and Hazel being presented as sophisticated women-of-the-world, but they broke the mould, in spite of the limitations imposed on them.

Proud, defiant, and militant, Hazel insisted on a clause in her movie contracts stating that she was not to be cast as piano-playing maids, and for a time this worked, and she worked. In films such as *Something to Shout About* (1943), *I Dood It* (1943), and *Broadway Rhythm* (1944), Hazel's chic appearances helped change the image of black women in American cinema. However, Hazel's movie career ended abruptly after an appearance in Warner Bros.' *Rhapsody in Blue* (1945), an all-star musical based on the life of the composer George Gershwin. During the filming of Columbia's *The Heat's On* (1943) starring Mae West, Hazel went on strike and held up the production for three days. There were eight black girls dancing in Hazel's musical number, and they were supposed to see eight black guys off to war while Hazel, dressed as a member of the Women's Army Corps (WAC), performed at the piano. During the filming of this number, Hazel lost her temper when the makeup man was ordered to spray the girls' aprons with oil and dirt: "I blew sky high," she later recalled in *Notes and Tones — Musician-to-Musician Interviews* (1993), "I honestly did. I said 'How can you think that young women are going to see their sweethearts off to war wearing dirty aprons?' I finally got them paid as dress extras, and they wore their own clothes. It held up the production for three days. They told me I would never make another picture. I was under contract for one more, *Rhapsody in Blue*, and when that was finished, I never did make another picture in Hollywood." It was Harry Cohn, head of Columbia, who ended Hazel's film career for holding up the production of *The Heat's On*. After *Rhapsody in Blue*, Hazel did not work in Hollywood again. Meanwhile, Lena Horne remained under contract to M-G-M until 1950, and made a number of successful appearances in the early years (1942-46), but after 1946 the studio seemed to lose interest in her and she made only two films: *Words and Music* (1948) and *Duchess of Idaho* (1950), unlike other M-G-M contract players who worked all the time.

Unlike Lena and Hazel, others, who had spent many years playing bit roles as maids, and occasionally broke the mould, have never been acknowledged. From 1930 to 1958, Theresa Harris appeared in more than seventy films. She is best remembered for playing Bette Davis's lively maid Zette in *Jezebel* (1938), but Theresa should be acknowledged for her role as Alma, the West Indian servant girl, in the "horror" classic *I Walked with a Zombie* (1943). Produced by Val Lewton and directed by Jacques Tourneur, the screenplay was loosely based on Charlotte Bronte's novel *Jane Eyre*. It is an atmospheric tale of voodoo and forbidden love set on an island in the Caribbean. Alma, and another black character, the calypso singer played by Sir Lancelot, who acts as a "Greek chorus", stand out because they are humanized by Tourneur and do not speak in the "Negro" dialect expected from black characters in Hollywood movies at that time. Tourneur later reflected, in an unidentified interview, "I have always refused to caricature black people. I have never, or hardly ever, showed them in the role of servants. I have always endeavoured to give them a profession, to have them speak normally rather than for some comic effect. I have often been accused of being a 'nigger lover' and for many months I was kept away from the studios for that very reason. It was a kind of grey list."

Another rare example of this kind of 'humanizing' of the Hollywood caricature is the classic *It's a Wonderful Life* (1946), directed by Frank

Capra and starring James Stewart. The veteran character actress Lillian Randolph plays a maid but she is very much a member of the family who employ her. As Annie, Randolph speaks her mind to her employers, the Baileys, and it is impossible to imagine Ma Bailey (Beulah Bondi) treating her as anything less than an equal. Like Alma in *I Walked with a Zombie*, Annie is treated with respect, and beautifully integrated into the plot, but such examples are rare. In the 1940s, when Nina Mae returned to Hollywood, mostly the roles for black actresses were one-dimensional stereotypes and could be painful experiences for the actresses who played them. When the jazz singer Billie Holiday went to Hollywood in 1947 to make a movie called *New Orleans* she was excited. Holiday had been a life-long fan of Hollywood movies, and thought she was going to play herself in it and to sing a few songs, like Lena Horne and Hazel Scott were doing in their films. Holiday felt humiliated when she discovered she had to play a maid. She later complained in her autobiography, *Lady Sings the Blues* (1956): "You just tell me one Negro girl who's made movies who didn't play a maid or a whore. I don't know any. I found out I was going to do a little singing, but I was still playing the part of a maid. I never made another movie. And I'm in no hurry."

Nina Mae's "comeback" film was an atmospheric melodrama called *Dark Waters* (1944) starring Merle Oberon and directed by Andre de Toth. Though unappreciated at the time of its release, *Dark Waters* is now recognised as one of the better gothic melodramas of the 1940s. Oberon's biographers, Charles Higham and Roy Moseley, also acknowledged her fine performance under de Toth's direction. They wrote in *Merle — A Biography of Merle Oberon* (1983): "Merle gave one of her best performances in *Dark Waters*: sensitive, delicately shaded, excellent in the scene of hysteria in the beginning. The direction has great gothic flair, using all-out melodramatic effects."

Nina Mae was cast in a supporting role as a maid, but thankfully the maid was not one dimensional. The role was small, and Nina Mae was not as slim and pretty as she had been in the 1930s, but the actress infused Florella with her own attractive personality. She also succeeded in doing this in her next film, the comedy *Together Again* (1944) starring Irene Dunne. Nina Mae had a small, uncredited role as Dunne's maid. Lawrence F. LaMar noted in *The Chicago Defender* (November 18, 1944) that the former star "was most strikingly beautiful in *Dark Waters* and her voice registered perfectly. The same was noted in the lengthy scene she appeared in *Together Again*. In both pictures, Miss McKinney essays the role of a maid…She is actually refreshing in the minor roles, making them stand out. Her diction should forever convince Hollywood that it is not necessary to make Negro characters use southern dialect in order to establish their racial identity."

Following *Dark Waters* and *Together Again* there were only occasional small roles as maids, mostly uncredited, until she was given a featured role in *Pinky* (1949). In the thriller *The Power of the Whistler* (1945), starring Richard Dix, Nina Mae is cast in another uncredited role, as Flotilda, maid to Constantina, played by Tala Birell. In *Night Train to Memphis* (1946), she is just listed on the cast list as "maid". The mystery drama *Danger Street* (1947), starring the 1930s child star Jane Withers, was directed by Lew Landers who had already directed Nina Mae in *The Power of the Whistler*. Nina Mae plays a character called Veronica, presumably a maid.

Nina Mae's penultimate film was 20th Century-Fox's *Pinky* (1949), produced by Darryl F. Zanuck, one of Hollywood's top moguls and a popular showman. Unlike other heads of Hollywood studios in the 1940s, in addition to making popular entertainment, Zanuck wanted to make movies that had a "social conscience". In 1947 he received an Oscar for best film for *Gentleman's Agreement*, one of the first films to explore anti-semitism in America. With an eye on the box office — and another Oscar — Zanuck decided to produce another film about a "forbidden" subject, saying, "Let's do it again with a Negro." The result was *Pinky*. In fact, in 1949 and 1950, four other landmark films attempted to take seriously America's "race" problem: *Home of the Brave* (1949), *Lost Boundaries* (1949), *Intruder in the Dust* (1949) and *No Way Out* (1950), in which Sidney Poitier made a memorable film debut. Before the end of the 1950s he had become one of the first African American screen actors to achieve star status in Hollywood, and he was the first to be nominated for a best actor Oscar (for *The Defiant Ones*, 1958).

The so-called "race problem" films suggested a trend toward black realism in American cinema, but compromises were made, including the casting of the lead character in 20th Century-Fox's *Pinky*. If a black actress had been cast in *Pinky* as the light-skinned, Southern-born Patricia "Pinky" Johnson, who passes for white while training as a nurse in the North, it might have atoned for Hollywood's almost nonexistent depiction of black women since the war. In spite of her fame and popularity, Lena Horne was overlooked for *Pinky*, a film that might have established her as a major movie star, and dramatic actress. Lena desperately wanted the part, as she later explained in her award-winning one-woman show *The Lady and Her Music* (1981), but on reflection it is doubtful that Lena could have been convincing as a black woman who could pass for white. A better choice would have been Hilda Simms, the Broadway star of the black-cast drama *Anna Lucasta*, produced by the American Negro Theatre company. In the end the role of Pinky went to a white 20th Century-Fox contract player, Jeanne Crain. The only whiter actress under contract to the studio at that time was Betty Grable. Crain was probably cast for shock value, because her screen persona was the pretty, wholesome girl-next-door in films like *State Fair* (1945). She couldn't have been further from anyone's casting expectations, but surprisingly, in spite of her limitations as an actress, Crain is very good in the role. The film's director, Elia Kazan, later reflected in Jeff Young's *Kazan on Kazan* (1999): "Jeanne Crain was a sweet girl, but she was like a Sunday school teacher. I did my best with her, but she didn't have any fire. The only good thing about her face was that it went so far in the direction of no temperament that you felt Pinky was floating through all of her experiences without reacting to them, which is what 'passing' is."

In *Pinky*, Patricia Johnson returns to her home in the South having spent years training to be a nurse in the North. Home is a shack on the outskirts of a black shantytown, where her granny, a matriarch known in the local community as Aunt Dicey (played by Ethel Waters), works as a washerwoman. For years she has undertaken backbreaking work to pay for granddaughter's training. Dicey also takes care of a sick elderly white woman, Miss Em (played by Ethel Barrymore), who has a paternalistic respect for "Negroes." Dicey realises that Pinky has been passing for white, which she angrily claims is a "sin against God." After facing up to her grandmother's anger, Pinky is exposed to racism and various indignities including an attempted rape by two drunken white men, before finding happiness within herself — as a black woman.

Nina Mae was cast in an unsympathetic supporting role as Rozelia, a razor-toting whore from the shantytown. After Pinky has confronted the con man Jake Walters (Frederick O'Neal) about some money he has stolen from her grandmother, he takes the money from Rozelia's purse, and gives it to Pinky. There is no evidence that Jake and Rozelia are married, but when he takes her purse from a drawer in the bedroom of his home, it can be assumed that the couple are living in "sin". This is in keeping with the image of Jake and Rozelia as the shanty town's "low life", a direct contrast to the respectable and God-fearing Dicey Johnson. When Rozelia wrongly suspects that Pinky is fraternizing with Jake, she attacks Pinky outside Jake's house. Unfortunately the attack is witnessed by two local white police officers, who arrest Pinky, Jake and Rozelia.

For Nina Mae, this was a sad finale to the film career that had been launched so successfully twenty years earlier with *Hallelujah*. Her beauty had faded, and so had the sense of fun she displayed ten years earlier in *Gang Smashers* (see Chapter 5). Nina Mae was no longer the sophisticated, husky voiced entertainer of the 1930s. When she filmed *Pinky* she was still only thirty-six, but she looked much older.

The African American film historian Donald Bogle later commented on Nina Mae's role in *Pinky* in his book *Toms, Coons, Mulattoes, Mammies & Bucks* (1973): "Though she was effective, the part did little for her career, and it was hard to believe that the stocky, bleary-eyed harridan on screen had once been the bright-eyed, carefree Chick [in *Hallelujah*]."

Elia Kazan was unhappy with *Pinky* and claimed only his first film, *A Tree Grows in Brooklyn* (1945), to be the best among his early work. Several of his post-*Pinky* films, including *A Streetcar Named Desire* (1951) and *On the Waterfront* (1954), for which he won his second Oscar, eclipsed his earlier films. But Kazan's dismissal of *Pinky* (he later said "it was a pastiche, taking a subject that was dynamite and castrating it") in various biographies and his own autobiography undermines the film's importance. Admittedly *Pinky* lacks the documentary realism of *Intruder in the Dust*, and as a Hollywood drama about racism in America it is not as powerful as *No Way Out*. But in 1949, *Pinky*'s setting and characters departed from Hollywood's sentimental and stereotypical vision of the South and race relations. *Gone with the Wind*, with its devoted slaves, had been made only ten years earlier, and *Song of the South*, with Uncle Remus telling delightful stories about Brer Rabbit and singing "Zip a Dee Doo Dah" was released just three years earlier. Compared to these movies, *Pinky* is a radical departure for Hollywood, in spite of the film's compromises and casting of a white actress in the lead.

The five films in the "race problem" cycle were all well received by movie critics, but *Pinky* was the biggest moneymaker, trailing *Jolson Sings Again* as the top moneymaking film of 1949. None of the other "race problem" films made it into the top twenty. However, *Pinky* did not repeat the success of Zanuck and Kazan's *Gentleman's Agreement* at the Academy Awards. There was no best picture nomination, though Jeanne Crain was nominated for best actress, a triumph for the young star who had defied her critics and transformed herself from girl next door to impressive dramatic actress. She lost out to Olivia de Havilland in *The Heiress*. *Pinky*'s two Ethels, Barrymore and Waters, were both nominated for best supporting actress.

It is hardly worth mentioning Nina Mae's final film, the western *Copper Canyon* (1950) starring Ray Milland. Her uncredited role as Hedy Lamarr's maid Theresa was so brief, if you blinked, you missed her.

CHAPTER 8

WHAT HAPPENED
TO
NINA MAE?

1950-1967

AFTER APPEARING IN THE FILMS *PINKY* (1949) AND *Copper Canyon* (1950), the rest of Nina Mae's life has remained something of a mystery. Very little information has surfaced, but what has been made available suggests that her final years were difficult and painful. Unconfirmed reports suggest that she became an alcoholic and drug addict, and her physical appearance in *Pinky* may confirm this. After the 1930s her career went into decline. In the 1940s she was a former movie star who had ended up serving white movie stars, an unbearable humiliation. In the 1950s there was little, or no, work. Nina Mae's tragic downfall could have been due to a combination of frustration with her career, and her dependence on alcohol and drugs.

In October 1949 it was reported in several newspapers that Nina Mae had filed a $700,000 damage suit against the African American *Ebony* magazine charging that one of its recent articles "defamed her and held her up to ridicule."

In 1951 Nina Mae made what was to be her last recorded professional appearance. Harlem's famous Apollo Theatre on 125th Street, which was famous for providing African American audiences with the best of black entertainment, decided to try something different. They staged productions of Sidney Kingsley's *Detective Story*, starring Sidney Poitier, and W. Somerset Maugham's *Rain*. The latter starred Nina Mae as Sadie Thompson, a smoking, drinking, jazz listening prostitute who had been portrayed in films by Gloria Swanson and Joan Crawford. However, this venture was not a success and the Apollo Theatre's co-owner, Frank Schiffman, cancelled plans to stage two additional dramas. He complained that black audiences did not care for drama, but theatre veterans took exception to Schiffman.

In his survey of "The Negro Theatre and the Harlem Community", published in an anthology entitled *Harlem, U. S. A.* (1964), edited by John Henrik Clarke, Loften Mitchell commented: "In the midst of what Harlemites considered a new Renaissance, the Apollo Theatre sponsored two shabby productions of 'white' plays with Negro actors. Both productions were artistically and commercially unsuccessful. The Apollo's management stated publicly that Harlemites did not care for serious drama. The Council on the Harlem Theatre issued a statement declaring: 'The owner of the Apollo has insulted the Negro people by bringing to this community two inferior pieces with little meaning to our lives. Ridiculous prices were charged.'" Mitchell added that the failure of these two productions served as a catalyst for the staging of productions by African American authors at various Harlem venues.

For Sidney Poitier, a young actor on the look-out for interesting work, but at that time spending more time waiting for his agent to call than actually acting, *Detective Story* was a positive experience. In his autobiography, *This Life* (1980), he recalled: "Rehearsals were a joy. I was happy to be back in action again, and especially so with a group of dedicated black actors who were pouring their creative energy into our uptown production, giving it a different kind of liveliness from what it had had on Broadway. All in all, and critical reactions notwithstanding, it was an enriching experience doing a dramatic play at the Apollo Theatre , whose audience, since time immemorial, was used to big bands, rhythm and blues, Ella Fitzgerald, Billy Eckstine, and Pigmeat Markham's vaudeville comedy sketches."

In 1953 *Jet* magazine reported in its February 5 issue: "Oldtime vaudeville and movie star Nina Mae McKinney is spending $1,000 for sexy gowns she will wear when she launches her comeback at Small's Paradise as the star of Manhattan Paul's revue."

In 1954, the year in which Dorothy Dandridge enjoyed success with her triumphant appearance in *Carmen Jones*, a sad looking Nina Mae was featured in the February issue of *Hue* magazine. An article entitled "What Happened to: Nina Mae McKinney?" revealed a still-young at forty-two Nina Mae looking much older, overweight, and unrecognisable as the once breathtakingly beautiful young star of the 1930s. The magazine claimed that, after appearing in *Pinky*, the actress had "closed the door" on her acting and singing career: "She virtually retired to Harlem, shunned entertainment floodlights for three years. Today. Nina Mae is preparing a return to show business in a new act with ex-Count Basie guitarist, Jimmy McLin, hopes it will return her to stardom." However, stardom eluded her, and this appears to be her last attempt at a show business "comeback". *Jet* magazine (February 4, 1954) noted that Nina Mae "will break in her new act on a USO tour of Japan. She plays the guitar."

Occasionally fragments and snippets of information surfaced about Nina Mae throughout the 1950s and 1960s. In the 1950s Ethel Waters and Billie Holiday published autobiographies which became best-sellers, and Nina Mae appears to have wanted to do the same. In their issue dated February 13, 1958, *Jet* magazine briefly reported that the "ex-movie actress is trying to peddle her life story to a book publisher. In the story she tells why she couldn't get movie work when she refused to "act right" with certain wolfish producers." Sadly, no autobiography was forthcoming. On July 20, 1960 Dorothy Kilgallen wrote in her column "The Voice of Broadway" in *The Cosholton Tribune* (Cosholton, Ohio) that "One-time movie star Nina Mae McKinney is seriously ill in Harlem Hospital. She could use friends right now." Seven years later, Nina Mae died.

Nina Mae's death at the age of fifty-four on May 3, 1967 passed virtually unnoticed. There was no acknowledgement of her death in the obituary page of the famous show business trade newspaper *Variety*, but a short obituary did appear in the *Amsterdam News* on Saturday May 13, 1967. It noted that Nina Mae had died of a heart attack on Wednesday May 3 in New York's Metropolitan Hospital, and her remains were at Odessa M. Bailey Funeral Home until Monday May 8 where she was viewed by hundreds of people who had known or who had heard of the famed star of stage, screen and radio. The obituary also described her funeral at The Little Church Around the Corner on East 29th Street, near Fifth Avenue, at 8pm on the evening of Monday May 8. Fellow members of the Negro Actors Guild and friends attended. The body was cremated at Ferncliff on Tuesday May 9. The obituary writer also noted that "Miss McKinney is survived by an aunt, Mrs. Alice Crawford and a cousin, Mrs. Robert Foster." Nina Mae's death certificate, filed in the City of New York's Vital Records department, makes for depressing reading. According to the certificate, Nina Mae was widowed; her occupation is listed as "domestic"; and the business or industry in which she was employed was recorded as "private families." Says Charlene Regester in *African American Actresses — The Struggle for Visibility, 1900-1960* (2010): "There was no mention that she had been an actress in Hollywood. Most disturbing is that in spite of her talent and her desire to become a prominent screen actress, in death she was reduced to the very role that she had attempted to escape, that of a domestic servant." According to Donald Bogle in *Bright Boulevards, Bold Dreams — The Story of Black Hollywood* (2005): "A technician from *Hallelujah* recalled attending a dinner party in New York where he was served by an obese and blowzy maid who looked familiar to him. He was shocked to realize it was Nina Mae McKinney. True or not, the story became part of McKinney's legend."

In 1976, in a *Cinema* magazine special edition entitled "Women and Film", Nina Mae was celebrated alongside such important names as the silent screen star Blanche Sweet; actress and screenwriter Ruth Gordon; film editor Verna Fields; and director Lina Wertmuller. Nina Mae's tribute was a two-spread featuring mostly stills from *Hallelujah* and the poster from *Gang Smashers*. The text was written by the African American actress Frances E. Williams, who explained that Nina Mae's early success was short lived: "There were no leading roles for Black ladies."

In 1978, probably due to Donald Bogle's enthusiastic appraisal of her screen work earlier in the decade, Nina Mae's contribution to cinema was recognised with a posthumous award from America's Black Film-makers Hall of Fame. In addition to this, her appearance in the BBC's *Television Demonstration Film* of 1937 has assured her a place in British television history. Just about every documentary that acknowledges the early, pre-war days of the BBC's television service, including *The Birth of Television* (BBC, 1977), *Magic Rays of Light* (BBC, 1981) and *The A to Z of Television* (Channel 4, 1990), includes the footage of the radiant and charismatic Nina Mae singing "Papa Tree Top Tall".

When Donald Bogle acknowledged and appraised the early black stars of Hollywood in his book *Toms, Coons, Mulattoes, Mammies & Bucks* (1973), he singled out Nina Mae for special praise: "Much that she experimented with in *Hallelujah* — the hands on the hips, the hard-as-nails brassy voice — was to become stock in trade for black leading ladies. One merely has to view Dorothy Dandridge's entrance in *Carmen Jones* with her particular type of sensual swagger to realise that other actresses picked up McKinney's techniques. At times even Jean Harlow appeared as if she had learned something about rough nightlife heroines from her. Nina Mae McKinney's final contribution to the movies now lay in those she influenced."

In 2005, in *Stepin' Fetchit — The Life and Times of Lincoln Perry*, Mel Watkins offered a revealing assessment of Nina Mae's brief, but memorable Hollywood career:

"On some levels, McKinney broke the colour line in Hollywood; before her no black performer had been courted with such uninhibited exuberance. Immediately after the release of *Hallelujah* she was hailed as "the greatest acting discovery of the age" by Irving Thalberg, M-G-M's second-in-command and one of the most powerful and respected producers in Hollywood. She quickly became a media darling as well as a frequent guest at Hollywood's most elite affairs…McKinney was being touted as a fast-rising star who combined the exoticism of Josephine Baker with the exuberance, sensuality, raw sex appeal, and liberated spirit of Clara Bow, the "It Girl"…By the spring of 1930, however, Hollywood's love affair with the "bronze" Lolita had noticeably cooled. Shortly after signing with M-G-M, she shot *They Learned About Women*, a mediocre musical that was universally panned. But McKinney's charismatic performance as a chorus-line singer in the "Harlem Madness" sequence was cheered by most critics…but after all was said and done, the film colony's infatuation with the young starlet seems to have been more libidinal than professional…there was no room for a Negro siren or leading lady in Hollywood feature films during the thirties."

APPENDIX

Richard Watts, Jr., "Sight and Sound",
New York Herald Tribune (June 17, 1934)

Appearing at the Femina, the swanky night club of Athens, (Yes — I'm in Athens) is a performer who is billed as "The Black Greta Garbo." As an earnest heroine-worshipper, who is interested in Garbos of any hue, I naturally gave up plans for climbing to the Acropolis to seek out this enthusiastically acclaimed lady, and discovered to my surprise that her right to the title is far more legitimate than is the custom in such matters. For it turns out that her name is Nina Mae McKinney, and unless your memory in cinematic matters is lamentably brief, you will recall her as the beautiful and talented Negro girl who gave such a magnificent performance in the leading role in "Hallelujah," the first distinguished talking picture, a film which stands with "All Quiet on the Western Front" as a pioneer classic of this still unsurveyed new dramatic medium. Being a rival of Aldous Huxley and Queen Victoria as a traveler who finds moral lessons in distant scenes, I cannot help suggesting that her far removed absence from the Hollywood that should be finding vehicles for this striking girl's authentic talents is as scornful a comment on our national artistic life as the fact that "Men in White" should be sought out for Pulitzer acclaim in preference to the vastly superior "Yellow Jack."

Anyway, Miss McKinney's genuinely brilliant performance in "Hallelujah" secured for her, not film stardom, but a minor role in a Dorothy Mackaill film and then a few appearances in motion picture shorts that no one ever saw. It seems, however, that Europe has been more interested in a performer who, with Ethel Waters, shares the position of legitimate successor to the eminent Florence Mills. A success in the night clubs of London, the heroine of "Hallelujah" has been equally triumphant in her appearances in Paris, Budapest and Dublin, a city which, being a sensible young woman, she likes tremendously. Now in the Greek capital, she is not only very definitely the belle of the excellent bar at the Hotel Grand Bretagne, the finest cocktail spot in the Near East, but is the bright, outstanding star of the Athenian night life. Yet it is indicative that the song in "As Thousands Cheer,"* which represents Josephine Baker — a player definitely inferior to Miss McKinney, by the way — as sighing wistfully for Harlem is telling the truth that the truth of Athenian gaiety, who is greeted everywhere with honors in this Levantine metropolis, is enormously anxious to get back to the unappreciative United States. Meanwhile she is planning, after leaving Athens late in June, to appear in a British motion picture. There is a possibility, too, of her appearing on the London stage in a revival of "Lulu Belle."

It seems that the Near East is the limbo for screen stars who are not active in Hollywood these days. Most of them are not triumphant and in the flesh as in the case of Nina Mae McKinney, whose exile from the cinema is the result entirely of narrow and intolerant racial matters.

Richard Watts, Jr. is referring to Irving Berlin's "Harlem on My Mind" which he wrote for Ethel Waters to sing in his Broadway revue As Thousands Cheer (1933).

FILMOGRAPHY

FEATURE FILMS

Hallelujah (1929)
M-G-M. King Vidor (DIRECTOR). Wanda Tuchock (SCREENPLAY). King Vidor (STORY). Gordon Avil (CINEMATOGRAPHY). Cedric Gibbons (ART DIRECTOR). Eva Jessye (MUSICAL DIRECTOR).

Nina Mae McKinney sings "Swanee Shuffle" (Irving Berlin).

Cast includes Daniel L. Haynes (Zeke), Nina Mae McKinney (Chick), William E. Fountaine (Hot Shot), Harry Gray (Parson), Fannie Belle de Knight (Mammy), Everett McGarrity (Spunk), Victoria Spivey (Missy Rose), Milton Dickerson, Robert Couch, Walter Tait (Johnson kids), Evelyn Pope Burwell, Eddie Connors (singers), and the Dixie Jubilee Singers.

They Learned About Women (1930)
M-G-M. Jack Conway, Sam Wood (DIRECTORS). Arthur "Bugs" Baer (SCREENPLAY). Leonard Smith (CINEMATOGRAPHY). Cedric Gibbons (ART DIRECTOR).

Nina Mae McKinney sings "Harlem Madness" (LYRICS: Jack Yellen, MUSIC: Milton Ager).

Cast includes Joseph T. Schenck (Jack Glennon), Gus Van (Jerry Burke), Bessie Love (Mary Collins), Mary Doran (Daisy Gebhart), J. C. Nugent (Stafford), Benny Rubin (Sam Goldberg), Tom Dugan (Tim O'Connor), Eddie Gribbon (Brennan), Francis X. Bushman, Jr. (Haskins), and Nina Mae McKinney ("Harlem Madness" singer).

Safe in Hell (British title: *The Lost Lady*) (1931)
First National. William A. Wellman (DIRECTOR). Barney "Chick" McGill (CINEMATOGRAPHY).

Nina Mae McKinney sings "When it's Sleepy Time Down South" (LYRICS: Clarence Muse, MUSIC: Leon Rene and Otis Rene)

Cast includes Dorothy Mackaill (Gilda Karlson), Donald Cook (Carl), Ralf Harolde (Piet), John Wray (Egan), Ivan Simpson (Crunch), Victor Varconi

(Gomez), Morgan Wallace (Bruno), Nina Mae McKinney (Leonie), Gustav Von Seyffertitz (Larson), Cecil Cunningham (Angie), Charles Middleton (Jones), Noble Johnson (Bobo), George Marion, Sr. (Jack), and Clarence Muse (Newcastle).

Kentucky Minstrels (1934)

Real Art Productions. Julius Hagen (PRODUCER). John Baxter (DIRECTOR). C. Denier Warren, John Watt and Harry S. Pepper (SCREENPLAY). Based on the BBC radio series *Kentucky Minstrels.* Sydney Blythe (CINEMATOGRAPHY). James A. Carter (ART DIRECTOR).

Nina Mae McKinney sings "I'm in Love With the Band" with Debroy Somers and his Band.

Cast includes [Harry] Scott and [Eddie] Whaley (Mott and Bayley), C. Denier Warren (Danny Goldman), April Vivian (Maggie), Wilson Coleman (Ben), Madge Brindley (Landlady), Roddy Hughes (Town Clerk), Norman Green (Massa Johnson), Harry S. Pepper and His White Coons, Polly Ward, Nina Mae McKinney, Eight Black Streaks, and Debroy Somers and his Band.

Reckless (1935)

M-G-M. David O. Selznick (PRODUCER). Victor Fleming (DIRECTOR). P. J. Wolfson (SCREENPLAY). George Folsey (CINEMATOGRAPHY). Cedric Gibbons, Merrill Pye and Edwin B. Willis (ART DIRECTORS).

Nina Mae McKinney and Jean Harlow sing "Reckless" (LYRICS: Jerome Kern, MUSIC: Oscar Hammerstein II).

Cast includes Jean Harlow (Mona), William Powell (Ned Riley), Franchot Tone (Bob Harrison), May Robson (Granny), and Nina Mae McKinney (herself).

Sanders of the River (1935)

London Films. Alexander Korda (PRODUCER). Zoltan Korda (DIRECTOR). Lajos Biro and Jeffrey Dell (SCREENPLAY). Based on the novel by Edgar Wallace. Georges Perinal (CINEMATOGRAPHY). Vincent Korda (ART DIRECTOR). Mischa Spoliansky (MUSIC). Arthur Wimperis (LYRICS).

Nina Mae McKinney sings "Little Black Dove" (LYRICS: Arthur Wimperis, MUSIC: Mischa Spoliansky).

Cast includes Paul Robeson (Bosambo), Leslie Banks (Commissioner Sanders), Nina Mae McKinney (Lilongo), Robert Cochran (Lieutenant Tibbetts), Martin Walker (Ferguson), Richard Grey (Hamilton), Tony Wane (King Mofolaba), Marquis de Portago (Farini), Eric Maturin (Smith), Allan Jeayes (Father O'Leary), Charles Carson (Governor of the Territory), Oboja (Chief of the Acholi Tribe), Orlando Martins (K'Lova), Luao and Kilongalonga (Chiefs of the Wagenia Tribe), Bertrand Frazer (Makara), James Solomon (Kaluba), Beresford Gale (Topolaka), Anthony Papafio (Bosambo's son), Deara Williams (Bosambo's daughter), John Thomas (Abiboo), Jomo Kenyatta (extra), and members of the Acholi, Sesi, Tefik, Juruba, Mendi and Kroo Tribes.

BBC — *The Voice of Britain* (1935)
GPO Film Unit. John Grierson (PRODUCER). Stuart Legg (DIRECTOR).

Nina Mae McKinney sings "Dinah" (Akst-Lewis-Young).

Cast includes H. M. George V, Queen Mary, Stanley Baldwin, H. G. Wells, George Bernard Shaw, Adrian Boult, Henry Hall and the BBC Dance Hall Orchestra, J. B. Priestley, G. K. Chesterton, Val Gielgud, George Lansbury, John Reith (voice), Nina Mae McKinney, and Garland Wilson.

Television Demonstration Film (1937)
BBC. Dallas Bower (PRODUCER AND DIRECTOR).

Nina Mae McKinney sings "Papa Tree Top Tall".

Cast includes Leslie Mitchell, Jasmine Bligh and Elizabeth Cowell (commentary), Sidonie Goossens, Charlotte Wolff, George Robey, Ballet Rambert, Margot Fonteyn, Irene Prador, Frederick Ashton, Robert Helpmann, Johnny Nit, Prince Monolulu, and Nina Mae McKinney.

Gang Smashers (1938)
Million Dollar Productions/Toddy Pictures. George D. Ringer (ASSOCIATE PRODUCER). Leo C. Popkin (DIRECTOR). Phil Dunham and Hazel

Barnes Jameson (SCREENPLAY). Robert Cline (CINEMATOGRAPHY). Harry Reif (ART DIRECTOR). Phil Moore (MUSICAL DIRECTOR).

Nina Mae McKinney sings "I Just Can't See it Your Way".

Cast includes Nina Mae McKinney (Laura Jackson), J. Lawrence Criner (Gat Dalton), Monte Hawley (Lefty), Mantan Moreland (Gloomy), Reginald Fenderson (Nick), Edward Thompson (Doyle), Neva Peoples (cabaret entertainer), Bo Jenkins (cabaret entertainer), and Phil Moore and his Orchestra.

The Devil's Daughter (1938)
Domino Film Corporation. Arthur Leonard (PRODUCER AND DIRECTOR).

Cast includes Nina Mae McKinney (Isabelle Walton), Jack Carter (Philip Ramsay), Ida James (Sylvia Walton), Hamtree Harrington (Percy Jackson), Willa Mae Lane (Elvira), and Emmett "Babe" Wallace (John Lowden).

Straight to Heaven (1939)
Million Dollar Productions. Arthur Leonard (PRODUCER AND DIRECTOR).

Nina Mae McKinney sings "When the Dark Becomes Dawn" (LYRICS: Bob Maxwell, MUSIC: Josef Myrow)

Cast includes Nina Mae McKinney (Ida Williams), Jack Carter (Stanley), Percy Verwayen ("Lucky" John Simon), Jackie Ward (Jimmy Williams), Lionel Monagas (Joe Williams), Bernice Vincent (Helen), Pearl Bains (Millie), James Baskette (1st Detective), George Williams (2nd Detective), Musical Specialty (3 Peppers), and Dance Specialty (Millie and Bubbles).

Dark Waters (1944)
United Artists. Benedict Bogeaus (PRODUCER). Andre de Toth (DIRECTOR). John Mescall and Archie Stout (CINEMATOGRAPHY). Charles Odds (ART DIRECTION). Miklos Rozsa (MUSIC).

Cast includes Merle Oberon (Leslie Calvin), Franchot Tone (Dr. George Grover), Thomas Mitchell (Mr. Sydney), Fay Bainter (Aunt Emily), Elisha Cook Jr (Cleeve), John Qualen (Uncle Norbert), Rex Ingram (Pearson Jackson),

Nina Mae McKinney (Florella), Odette Myrtil (Mama Boudreaux), and Eugene Borden (Papa Boudreaux).

Together Again (1944)

Columbia. Virgina Van Upp (PRODUCER). Charles Vidor (DIRECTOR). Joseph Walker (CINEMATOGRAPHY). Stephen Goosson, Van Nest Polglase (ART DIRECTORS), Werner R. Heymann (MUSIC).

Cast includes Irene Dunne (Anne Crandall), Charles Boyer (Georeg Corday), Charles Coburn (Jonathan Crandall, Sr.), Mona Freeman (Diana Crandall), Jerome Courtland (Gilbert Parker), Elizabeth Patterson (Jessie), Charles Dingle (Morton Buchanan), and Nina Mae McKinney (Maid).

The Power of the Whistler (1946)

Leonard S. Picker (PRODUCER). Lew Landers (DIRECTOR). Aubrey Wisberg (SCREENPLAY). L. William O'Connell (CINEMATOGRAPHY), John Datu (ART DIRECTOR), Wilbur Hatch (MUSIC).

Cast includes Richard Dix (William Everest), Janis Carter (Jean Lane), Jeff Donnell (Frances 'Frankie' Lane), Tala Birell (Constantine Ivaneska), John Abbott (Kaspar Andropolous), Cy Kendall (Druggist), Murray Alper (Joe Blainey, the trucker), and Nina Mae McKinney (as Constantine's maid).

Night Train to Memphis (1946)

Republic. Lesley Selander (DIRECTOR).

Cast includes Roy Acuff, Allan "Rocky" Lane, Adele Mara, Irving Bacon, Nina Mae McKinney (Maid)

Danger Street (1947)

Paramount. Lew Landers (DIRECTOR). Winston Miller (SCREENPLAY).

Cast includes Jane Withers (Pat Marvin), Robert Lowery (Larry Burke), Bill Edwards (Sandy Evans), Elaine Riley (Cynthia Van Loan), Lyle Talbot (Charles Johnson), and Nina Mae McKinney (Veronica).

Pinky (1949)
20th Century-Fox. Darryl F. Zanuck (PRODUCER). Elia Kazan (DIRECTOR). Philip Dunne, Dudley Nichols (SCREENPLAY). Based on the novel *Quality* by Cid Ricketts Sumner. Joe MacDonald (CINEMATOGRAPHY). Lyle Wheeler, J. Russell Spencer (ART DIRECTORS). Alfred Newman (MUSIC).

Cast includes Jeanne Crain (Patricia 'Pinky' Johnson), Ethel Barrymore (Miss Em), Ethel Waters (Mrs. Dicey Johnson), William Lundigan (Dr. Thomas Adams), Basil Ruysdael (Judge Walker), Kenny Washington (Dr. Canady), Nina Mae McKinney (Rozelia), Frederick O'Neal (Jake Walters), Evelyn Varden (Melba Wooley), Raymond Greenleaf (Judge Shoreham), Dan Riss (Stanley), Arthur Hunnicutt (Police Chief), William Hansen (Mr. Goolby), and Everett Glass (Mr. Wooley).

Copper Canyon (1950)
Paramount. Mel Epstein (PRODUCER). John Farrow (DIRECTOR). Richard English and Jonathan Latimer (SCREENPLAY). Charles B. Lang, Jr. (CINEMATOGRAPHY). Franz Bachelin and Hans Dreier (ART DIRECTORS). Daniele Amfitheatrof (MUSIC).

Cast includes Ray Milland (Johnny Carter), Hedy Lamarr (Lisa Roselle), Macdonald Carey (Deputy Lane Travis), Mona Freeman (Caroline Desmond), Harry Carey, Jr. (Lieutenant Ord), Frank Faylen (Mullins), Hope Emerson (Ma Tarbet), and Nina Mae McKinney (Theresa, the maid).

SHORT FILMS

Pie Pie Blackbird (1932)
Vitaphone (Warner Bros.). Roy Mack (DIRECTOR). A. Dorian Otvos (SCREENPLAY). E. B. DuPar (CINEMATOGRAPHY).

Nina Mae sings "Everything I Have Belongs to You".

Cast includes Nina Mae McKinney, Nicholas Brothers (Fayard and Harold), and Eubie Blake and his Orchestra.

London's Famous Clubs and Cabarets (1933)
British Pathe

Nina Mae sings "Bring Back the Charleston".

The Black Network (1936)
Vitaphone (Warner Bros.). Roy Mack (DIRECTOR). A. Dorian Otvos (SCREENPLAY). Ray Foster (CINEMATOGRAPHY). Cliff Hess (SONGS).

Nina Mae sings "Half of Me Wants to Be Good" (Cliff Hess).

Cast includes Nina Mae McKinney, Nicholas Brothers (Fayard and Harold), Babe Wallace, Amanda Randolph (Mezzanine Johnson), Bill 'Basement' Brown (Brutus Johnson), Eddie Green, Thomas Chappelle, and The Washboard Serenaders.

NOTES ON NINA MAE McKINNEY'S FILMOGRAPHY

Nina Mae is often credited with an appearance in an independently produced, low-budget comedy called *Mantan Messes Up* (1946). It starred the popular African American comedy actor Mantan Moreland, famous for his appearances in the *Charlie Chan* film series. No prints of the film appear to have survived, but on posters that *have* survived are images of the film's "guest stars": Nina Mae in *Gang Smashers* (1938) and Lena Horne. It would be safe to assume that *Mantan Messes Up* incorporated extracts of Nina Mae in *Gang Smashers* and Lena Horne in her 1938 "race movie" *The Duke is Tops* to bolster the entertainment value of the film. Both productions were made by the same production company that released *Mantan Messes Up*. It seems highly unlikely that either star took part in the film. Lena Horne was then under contract to M-G-M.

Several sources claim that Nina Mae appeared in the following feature films, but these appearances have not been verified: Fox's *In Old Kentucky* (1935) with Bill "Bojangles" Robinson; a John Wayne western (for Republic) called *The Lonely Trail* (1936) (uncredited as "dancer"); and M-G-M's *Without Love* (1945) starring Katharine Hepburn. She has also been credited for three musical shorts, also unsubstantiated: *Manhattan Serenade* (1930); Vitaphone's *Passing the Buck* (1932), directed by Roy Mack, in which she sang "Tiger Rag"; and Paramount's *Broadway Highlights* (1935), in which she is supposed to have sung "Good for Nothin' Joe".

It is more than likely that her appearance in the now lost 1940s American film *Swanee Showboat* is an out-take from the 1934 British film *Kentucky Minstrels* in which she sang "I'm in Love With the Band". This is because the African American comedy team Scott and Whaley are also credited in the cast, and they were the stars of *Kentucky Minstrels* and did not return to the United States after they settled in Britain in 1909. The finale to *Kentucky Minstrels* featuring Scott and Whaley and Nina Mae was released in the USA in the 1930s as *Minstrel Days* (a poor videotape copy surfaced in the 1990s and has now been deposited in the National Film and Television Archive in Britain).

Nina Mae is credited for a low-budget but now lost British film called *On Velvet* (1938), and her name is mentioned in several contemporary reviews. One source claims she sang "Swanee River" while another describes the backdrop to her appearance in the BBC's 1937 *Television Demonstration Film*. It could be that *On Velvet* included an out-take from the 1937 BBC film in which Nina Mae sang "Papa Tree Top Tall", but without evidence, this cannot be verified. It would make sense, because the film has been described as a musical about the setting up of an amateur television station. Perhaps its director, Widgey Newman, "lifted" Nina Mae's sequence from the BBC film? A contemporary review in *To-Day's Cinema* (March 10, 1938) briefly mentions Nina Mae singing a "soulful song before impressionist backgrounds" as one of the stars of the film's "television show" but the same critic is not impressed with the film: "It is all somewhat of a hotchpotch, and not all of it even moderately entertaining."

Nina Mae did not appear in *St. Louis Gal,* a 1938 "race movie" for a company called the "Creative Cinema Corporation". Some sources have credited her for this film (for example David Meeker's 1981 book *Jazz in the Movies*), but it seems unlikely this production was ever filmed.

Though some sources claim that Nina Mae "ghosted" Jean Harlow's songs in M-G-M's *Reckless* (1935), it has now been established that the "ghost singer" was, in fact, Virginia Verrill, a singer who "dubbed" Harlow's vocals on other occasions, including M-G-M's *Suzy* (1936).

BIBLIOGRAPHY

James Baldwin, *The Devil Finds Work* (Michael Joseph, 1976)

Richard Barrios, *A Song in the Dark — The Birth of the Musical Film* (Oxford University Press, 1995)

Martin Bauml Duberman, *Paul Robeson* (The Bodley Head, 1989)

Donald Bogle and Rosalind Cash, "Is It Better to Be Shaft than Uncle Tom?" *The New York Times* (August 26, 1973), D11, D16.

Donald Bogle, *Toms, Coons, Mulattoes, Mammies & Bucks — An Interpretive History of Blacks in American Films* (Bantam Books, 1973)

Donald Bogle, *Brown Sugar — Eighty Years of America's Black Female Superstars* (Harmony Books, 1980)

Donald Bogle, *Blacks in American Films and Television — An Illustrated Encyclopedia* (Garland Publishing, 1988)

Donald Bogle, "The Defiant Ones — A Talk With Film Historian Donald Bogle." Interview with Lisa Jones. *Village Voice Film Special* (June 4, 1991), 67, 69, 88.

Donald Bogle, *Dorothy Dandridge — A Biography* (Amistad, 1997)

Donald Bogle, *Bright Boulevards, Bold Dreams — The Story of Black Hollywood* (One World/ Ballantine Books, 2005)

Donald Bogle, *Heat Wave — The Life and Career of Ethel Waters* (Harper, 2011)

Stephen Bourne, "Nina Mae McKinney", *Films in Review*, January/February 1991, Vol. XLII, No. 1/2

Stephen Bourne, "Denying Her Place — Hattie McDaniel's Surprising Acts" in Pam Cook and Philip Dodd, eds. *Women and Film — A Sight and Sound Reader* (Scarlet Press, 1993)

Stephen Bourne, *Black in the British Frame — The Black Experience in British Film and Television* (Continuum, 2001)

Stephen Bourne, *Elisabeth Welch — Soft Lights and Sweet Music* (Scarecrow Press, 2005)

Stephen Bourne, *Ethel Waters — Stormy Weather* (Scarecrow Press, 2007)

Stephen Bourne, *Butterfly McQueen Remembered* (Scarecrow Press, 2008)

Edwin M. Bradley, *The First Hollywood Musicals — A Critical Filmography of 171 Features, 1927 through 1932* (McFarland, 1996)

Geoff Brown with Tony Aldgate, *The Common Touch — The Films of John Baxter* (British Film Institute, 1989)

Kenneth M. Cameron, *Africa on Film — Beyond Black and White* (Continuum, 1994)

John Chilton, *Billie's Blues — A Survey of Billie Holiday's Career 1933-1959* (Quartet Books, 1975)

Champ Clark, *Shuffling to Ignominy — The Tragedy of Stepin Fetchit* (iUniverse, 2005)

Darlene Clark Hine, ed., *Facts On File Encyclopedia of Black Women in America — Theater Arts and Entertainment* (Facts On File, 1997)

Donald Clarke, *Wishing on the Moon — The Life and Times of Billie Holiday* (Viking, 1994)

Thomas Cripps, *Slow Fade to Black — The Negro in American Film 1900-1942* (Oxford University Press, 1977)

Nancy Dowd and David Shepherd, *King Vidor* (The Directors Guild of America and The Scarecrow Press, 1988)

Anna Everett, *Returning the Gaze — A Genealogy of Black Film Criticism, 1909-1949* (Duke University Press, 2001)

James Gavin, *Stormy Weather — The Life of Lena Horne* (Atria Books, 2009)

Leslie Gourse, ed., *The Billie Holiday Companion — Seven Decades of Commentary* (Omnibus Press, 1997)

Thomas Hischak, *The Oxford Companion to the American Musical* (Oxford University Press, 2008)

Billie Holiday with William Dufty, *Lady Sings the Blues* (Doubleday, 1956)

Herbert Howe, "A Jungle Lorelei", *Photoplay*, July 1929

Langston Hughes and Milton Meltzer, *Black Magic — A Pictorial History of the African-American in the Performing Arts* (Prentice-Hall, 1967)

Langston Hughes, *The Collected Works of Langston Hughes Volume 8 — The Later Simple Stories* (University of Missouri Press, 2001)

G. William Jones, *Black Cinema Treasures — Lost and Found* (University of North Texas, 1991)

John Kisch and Edward Mapp, *A Separate Cinema — Fifty Years of Black Cast Posters* (The Noonday Press, 1992)

Arthur Knight, *Disintegrating the Musical — Black Performance and the American Musical Film* (Duke University Press, 2002)

Eileen Landay, *Black Film Stars* (Drake Publishers, 1973)

Daniel J. Leab, *From Sambo to Superspade — The Black Experience in Motion Pictures* (Secker and Warburg, 1975)

Edward Mapp, *Directory of Blacks in the Performing Arts* (2nd ed.) (Scarecrow Press, 1990)

Frank Manchel, *Every Step a Struggle: Interviews with Seven Who Shaped the African-American Image in Movies* (New Academia Publishing, 2007)

Bob McCann, *Encyclopedia of African American Actresses in Film and Television* (McFarland 2010)

Douglas McVay, *The Musical Film* (A. Zwemmer, 1967)

David Meeker, *Jazz in the Movies* (Talisman Books, 1981)

Ethan Mordden, *The Hollywood Musical* (David and Charles, 1981)

Peter Noble, *The Negro in Films* (Skelton Robinson, 1948)

Gary Null, *Black Hollywood — The Negro in Motion Pictures* (The Citadel Press, 1975)

Charlene Regester, *African American Actresses — The Struggle for Visibility, 1900-1960* (Indiana University Press, 2010)

Henry T. Sampson, *Blacks in Black and White — A Source Book on Black Films* (2nd ed.) (Scarecrow Press, 1995)

Henry T. Sampson, *Swingin' on the Etherwaves — A Chronological History of African Americans in Radio and Television Broadcasting, 1925-1955* (Vol. 1 and 2) (Scarecrow Press, 2005)

William A. Shack, *Harlem in Montmarte — A Paris Jazz Story Between the Great Wars* (University of Califorina Press, 2001)

Barry Singer, *Black and Blue — The Life and Lyrics of Andy Razaf* (Schirmer Books, 1992)

Peter Stanfield, *Body and Soul — Jazz and Blues in American Film 1927-63* (University of Illinois Press, 2005)

Cobbett Steinberg, *Reel Facts — The Movie Records Books* (Vintage Books, 1982)

Frank T. Thompson, *William A. Wellman* (Scarecrow Press, 1983)

Susan Tully Boyle and Andrew Bunie, *Paul Robeson — The Years of Promise and Achievement* (University of Massachusetts Press, 2001)

Ken Vail, *Lady Day's Diary — The Life of Billie Holiday 1937-1959* (Castle Communications, 1996)

Constance Valis Hill, *Brotherhood in Rhythm — The Jazz Tap Dancing of the Nicholas Brothers* (Oxford University Press, 2000)

Mel Watkins, *On the Real Side — A History of African American Comedy from Slavery to Chris Rock* (Simon and Schuster, 1994) (revised 1999)

Mel Watkins, *Stepin Fetchit — The Life and Times of Lincoln Perry* (Pantheon Books, 2005)

Frances E. Williams, "Nina Mae McKinney — The Black Garbo", *Cinema* Number 35, 1976, pp18-19.

Linda Williams, *Playing the Race Card — Melodramas of Black and White from Uncle Tom to O. J. Simpson* (Princeton University Press, 2001)

INDEX

ABOUT THE AUTHOR

STEPHEN BOURNE GREW UP IN A SOCIAL HOUSING PROJECT in Peckham, south east London, and left school in 1974 at the age of sixteen with no qualifications. He describes his research methods as self-taught. In spite of his educationally disadvantaged background Stephen pursued the world of academia, and now has two degrees: a Bachelor of Arts (Hons) in Film and Television from the London College of Printing, awarded in 1988, and a Master of Philosophy from De Montfort University in Leicester, awarded in 2006.

In 1991 Stephen was a founder member of Britain's Black and Asian Studies Association and co-authored his first book, *Aunt Esther's Story*, with his adopted aunt, Esther Bruce (1912-1994). She was a black seamstress born in London in the Edwardian era. From 1989 to 1992 Stephen was employed by the British Film Institute and BBC as a researcher on *Black and White in Colour*, a ground-breaking project that unearthed the history of race and representation in British television.

Stephen is the author of two acclaimed histories of British popular cinema: *Brief Encounters*, a survey of lesbians and gays (Cassell, 1996) and the award-winning *Black in the British Frame — The Black Experience in British Film and Television* (Continuum, 2001).

Stephen is also the author of several biographies of African American divas including Adelaide Hall (*Sophisticated Lady — A Celebration of Adelaide Hall*, ECOHP, 2001); Elisabeth Welch (*Elisabeth Welch — Soft Lights and Sweet Music*, Scarecrow Press, 2005); and Ethel Waters (*Ethel Waters — Stormy Weather*, 2007). He has also written a biography of the actress Butterfly McQueen (*Butterfly McQueen Remembered*, Scarecrow Press, 2008), who was famous for playing Scarlett O'Hara's servant in the movie classic *Gone with the Wind* (1939).

Stephen's other books include several social histories of black people in Britain including *A Ship and a Prayer* (ECOHP, 1999); *Speak of Me As I Am — The Black Presence in Southwark Since 1600* (Southwark

Council, 2005); *Dr. Harold Moody* (Southwark Council, 2008) and *Mother Country — Britain's Black Community on the Home Front 1939-45* (The History Press, 2010).

He has also contributed to the *The Encyclopaedia of British Film* (2003) and *The Oxford Companion to Black British History* (2007).

For further information go to *www.stephenbourne.co.uk.*

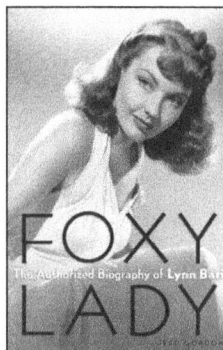

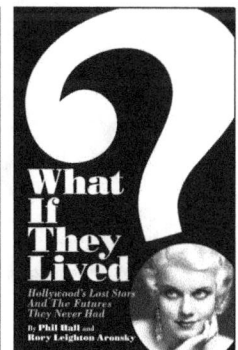